READING GROUP CHOICES
2014

*Selections for lively
book discussions*

20TH ANNIVERSARY EDITION

ISBN 9780975974292

For further information, contact:
Reading Group Choices
532 Cross Creek Court
Chester, MD 21619
Toll-free: 1-866-643-6883
info@ReadingGroupChoices.com
ReadingGroupChoices.com

Welcome to
READING GROUP *Choices*

Dear Friends,

2014 marks the **20th anniversary of Reading Group Choices.**
We have reason to celebrate!

So much has changed in the book business during the past twenty years. We have ever expanding options for enjoying great literature, from traditional print media to novels that are accessible through electronic sources. But whether you like to read with a tablet on a train or prefer a well broken in paperback in the bathtub, we all come together for one reason—it's simply about the love of a great book!

Truly, there is nothing like the comfort to be found in reading just the right novel, discovered at just the right time. Through a great book, you can learn so much about yourself and others; travel the world; and make friends that you never forget, both real and fictional. We are proud to introduce this current collection of wonderful books to inspire your book club toward meaningful and lively discussions.

As always, we would like to thank you, our readers, for supporting and inspiring us as we look forward to the future. Thank you as well to the many talented authors who contribute to our blogs and author interviews and to our many friends in the publishing industry.

Please visit us on-line at ReadingGroupChoices.com, on Facebook, Twitter, Pinterest, and through our new downloadable app.

Thank you for keeping the joy of reading alive!

READING GROUP CHOICES

Book Group Favorites

Early in 2013, we asked thousands of book groups to tell us what books they read and discussed during 2012 that they enjoyed most. The top ten titles were:

1. *Gone Girl* by Gillian Flynn (Crown)
2. *The Immortal Life of Henrietta Lacks* by Rebecca Skloot (Broadway)
3. *Unbroken* by Laura Hillenbrand (Random House Trade Paperbacks)
4. *Defending Jacob* by William Landay (Delacorte Press)
5. *The Paris Wife* by Paula McLain (Ballantine Books)
6. *The Language of Flowers* by Vanessa Diffenbaugh (Ballantine Books)
7. *Cutting for Stone* by Abraham Verghese (Vintage)
8. *Room* by Emma Donoghue (Little, Brown & Company)
9. *Still Alice* by Lisa Genova (Gallery)
10. *The Light Between Oceans* by M. L. Stedman (Scribner)
    The Hunger Games by Suzanne Collins (Scholastic Press)

Contents

GUIDELINES FOR
Lively Book Discussions

Respect space—Avoid "crosstalk" or talking over others.

Allow space—Some of us are more outgoing and others more reserved. If you've had a chance to talk, allow others time to offer their thoughts as well.

Be open—Keep an open mind, learn from others, and acknowledge there are differences in opinion. That's what makes it interesting!

Offer new thoughts—Try not to repeat what others have said, but offer a new perspective.

Stay on the topic—Contribute to the flow of conversation by holding your comments to the topic of the book.

Come find, friend, and follow us

On the web: **ReadingGroupChoices.com**

On our blog: **OntheBookcase.com**

On Facebook: **Reading Group Choices Fan Page**

On Twitter: **@ReadingGChoices**

On Pinterest: **Pinterest.com/ReadingGChoices**

THE AFFAIR

Colette Freedman

After eighteen years of marriage, Kathy Walker has settled into a pattern of comfortable routines—ferrying her two teenagers between soccer practice and piano lessons, running a film production business with her husband, Robert, and taking care of the beautiful Boston home they share. Then one day, Kathy discovers a suspicious number on her husband's phone. Six years before, Kathy accused Robert of infidelity—a charge he vehemently denied—and almost destroyed their marriage in the process.

Now Kathy must decide whether to follow her suspicions at the risk of losing everything, or trust the man with whom she's entwined her past, present, and future. As she grapples with that choice, she is confronted with surprising truths not just about her relationship, but about her friends, family, and her own motivations.

Skillfully crafted and deeply insightful, *The Affair* sensitively explores the complexities of love and the challenge of ever knowing another person fully, even as we endeavor to understand our own deepest longings.

*"Playwright Freedman presents a realistic and deft tale of infidelity, miscommunication, and conflicting emotions in her structurally compelling debut novel. In this resonant, enjoyable tale, Freedman demonstrates a keen understanding of relationships, and her formal choices enrich the narrative, allowing readers to sympathize with each character." —****Publishers Weekly***

ABOUT THE AUTHOR: **Colette Freedman** is an internationally produced playwright with over 15 produced plays, including *Sister Cities*, which was the hit of the 2008 Edinburgh Fringe. She has co-written, with international bestselling novelist Jackie Collins, the play *Jackie Collins Hollywood Lies*. In collaboration with the *New York Times* bestselling author Michael Scott, she has co-written the thriller *The Thirteen Hallows*.

February 2013 | Trade Paperback | Fiction | 336 pp | $15.00 | ISBN 9780758281005
Kensington Books | kensingtonbooks.com | colettefreedman.com

CONVERSATION STARTERS

1. Do you think Kathy violated Robert's trust by looking in his phone and checking his e-mails? Or do you think her actions were justified?

2. Kathy clearly states that she still feels sexy. Do you believe it is a false impression that it is usually men who are denied sex, when in fact it is often women who are sexually frustrated?

3. Rose tells Kathy, "Men stray. It's in their nature, whether we like it or not. It goes back to the time of cavemen. Men hunted and women nurtured. Tommy was just . . . hunting." Today's media often paints adultery as a defensible misdeed. Do you believe men cheat because they are wired to do so?

4. Do you agree with Rose's decision not to confront Tommy? Do you know women like Rose who have stood by quietly as their husbands cheated? What would you do in Rose's position?

5. Do you think Maureen, as Kathy's friend, had a responsibility to tell Kathy about Robert's affair? Or do you think Maureen's responsibility as Robert's secretary should be discretion? If you were in Maureen's position, what would you do?

6. At some point during the story, all three characters realize how similar Kathy and Stephanie look. Do you believe Robert's attraction to Stephanie is independent of Kathy, or tied up in his original feelings for her?

7. Stephanie is an extremely successful career woman. Do you think her ability to throw work Robert's way colored his relationship with her? Do you think their relationship would have lasted as long if she had stopped giving him work?

8. Do you think Stephanie and Robert could make it as a couple? Why do you believe Stephanie fell for Robert?

9. Do you think, despite his infidelity, Robert is a good father? Do you think he would want to have children with Stephanie?

10. Where do you see Robert in ten years? Who will he be with? Kathy? Stephanie? Someone else?

11. If you were Kathy, could you forgive Robert? In your opinion, should Kathy take Robert back? Why or why not?

12. Do you believe it is possible to love more than one person?

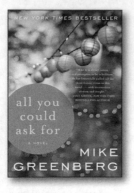

ALL YOU COULD ASK FOR

Mike Greenberg

Brooke has been happily married to her college sweetheart for fifteen years. Samantha's newly-wed bliss is steamrolled when she finds shocking evidence of infidelity on her husband's computer. Katherine works eighteen hours a day for the man who irreparably shattered her heart fifteen years ago. Brooke, Samantha, and Katherine don't know one another yet, but all three are about to discover the conquering power of friendship—and that they have all they could ask for, as long as they have each other.

*"Funny and moving." —**Connecticut Post***

*"Delves with authenticity and compassion into the lives and minds of three female characters. . . . This well-written page-turner by a surprising author . . . features true-to-life characters who are entertaining and compelling. A must read for fans of smart women's fiction." —**Library Journal***

*"Upbeat [and] snappy." —**Publishers Weekly***

*"The shared adversity these women face is portrayed realistically and tenderly . . . The three women are well drawn, and Greenberg displays an admirable ear for realistic dialogue. Fans of Deborah Copaken Konan, Sarah Pekkanen, and contemporary ensemble fiction will enjoy this debut novel." —**Booklist***

About the Author: **Mike Greenberg** is cohost of ESPN's *Mike & Mike* and the author of two previous *New York Times* bestsellers. He is a graduate of the Medill School of Journalism at Northwestern University and a native of New York City. He lives with his wife, Stacy, and their two children in Connecticut. In conjunction with the release of this book, Mike and Stacy have created a foundation called Heidi's Angels, through which all of the author's profits from the sale of this book will be donated to The V Foundation for Cancer Research to combat breast cancer.

September 2013 | Trade Paperback | Fiction | 288 pp | $14.99 | ISBN 9780062220769
William Morrow | harpercollins.com

CONVERSATION STARTERS

1. Would Samantha have become friends with Katherine and Brooke under different circumstances? What do the three women have in common besides the event that brings them together?

2. Samantha is horrified when she finds those pictures on Robert's laptop, but is she partially to blame for invading his privacy?

3. Brooke stakes much of her own happiness on her husband's satisfaction and his perception of her. Is this problematic?

4. Brooke says you need three core girlfriends: one who's like a sister, one who knows everything, and one a generation ahead of you. Do you agree? Who occupies these roles in your own life?

5. Robert seemed genuinely contrite when he went to see Samantha. Would you have taken him back? Why or why not?

6. Samantha is always trying to help people, and she wants to extend her generosity of spirit to Brooke. Do you think she was wrong in forcing Brooke to share her story? Was she at all motivated by guilt?

7. Why do you think Brook decides to do what she does? Do you agree with her choice? Do her loved ones deserve to be included in her decisions?

8. Brooke sees her life as divided into stages—her sweet sixteen, her wedding. What are the stages of your life?

9. Samantha reflects on her evening with Andrew Marks as "the night [she] learned that [she likes] being pretty." Despite confronting a serious life hurdle, she does not abandon her vanity. Is this something many women can relate to? What does being pretty mean to you?

10. Katherine and Samantha have a few "absolute deal-breakers"—a grown-up who calls his mother every day, a man who buys maxi pads for his dog. What are your absolute deal-breakers?

11. In her last person-to-person to Samantha, Brooke writes, "Please leave me alone." She tells her she'll be in touch when she's ready. What do you think ultimately moved her to reach out? What changed?

12. Brooke is the only one with a husband by her side, and yet she does not share her secret with him. Is she motivated by fear? Do you think that has more to do with her or with Scott?

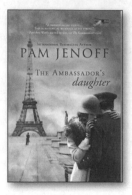

THE AMBASSADOR'S DAUGHTER

Pam Jenoff

Paris, 1919. The world's leaders have gathered to rebuild from the Great War. But for one woman, the City of Light harbors dark secrets and dangerous liaisons, for which many could pay dearly.

Brought to the peace conference by her father, a German diplomat, Margot Rosenthal initially resents being trapped in the French capital. But as she contemplates returning to Berlin and a life with Friedrich, the fiancé she hardly knows anymore, she decides that being in Paris is not so bad after all.

"A tale of surprise betrayals, unquenchable desire, and a necessary awakening, Jenoff's thorough and elaborate descriptions of character and setting makes for a satisfying period romance." —Publishers Weekly

"Fans of Kate Morton and Alyson Richman should reach for popular Jenoff's latest historical romance. . . . Jenoff ably plumbs the concepts of courage, faith and love against a dramatic backdrop." —Booklist

ABOUT THE AUTHOR: **Pam Jenoff** is the author of several novels, including *The Kommandant's Girl*, which received widespread acclaim, earned her a nomination for the Quill Awards, and became an international bestseller. She previously served as a Foreign Service Officer for the U.S. State Department in Europe, as the Special Assistant to the Secretary of the Army at the Pentagon, and as a practicing attorney at a large firm and in-house. She received her juris doctor from the University of Pennsylvania, her masters degree in history from Cambridge University, and her bachelors degree in international affairs from The George Washington University. Pam Jenoff lives with her husband and three children near Philadelphia where, in addition to writing, she teaches law school.

February 2013 | Trade Paperback | Fiction | 336 pp | $14.95 | ISBN 9780778315094
Harlequin MIRA | harlequin.com | pamjenoff.com

CONVERSATION STARTERS

1. As the story opens, Margot appears to be an independent and confident young woman. How do you think her character changes throughout the story, and what causes those changes? What did you feel was her greatest strength and weakness?

2. How do you think the loss of her mother affected Margot? How did this change throughout the book, particularly when she learned the truth?

3. Georg and Margot developed feelings for one another after mere days. What did you see in their time together that attracted them so powerfully? Do you believe it is possible to fall in love so quickly and for such a relationship to last?

4. Margot and Krysia became such close friends despite significant differences in age and circumstances. What do you think it was that drew them together, and what did each of them provide for the other? Have you ever found yourself in such a close but unlikely friendship?

5. Margot was a very young woman dealing with situations that most of us today would find completely overwhelming at age twenty. What do you think it was that Margot really wanted out of life?

6. What did you think about Margot's relationship with Stefan? Could you sympathize with her, being torn by an old promise to a man she didn't know anymore and her love for a man that offered her a promising future? What would you have done in her shoes?

7. Margot experienced anti-German sentiment from those around her who saw her as the enemy. Do you think this was a fair judgment, given the political climate of the time? Do you think this type of mentality still exists today?

8. Do you agree that Margot's relationship with her father improved over the course of the novel? How so, or how not?

9. *The Ambassador's Daughter* is the prequel to two of Pam Jenoff's other novels, *The Kommandant's Girl* and *The Diplomat's Wife*. If you have read those, how did you feel this book compared? Did knowing what happens twenty years down the line color your reading of this book?

THE ART FORGER

B. A. Shapiro

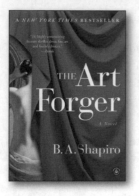

Almost twenty-five years after the infamous art heist at the Isabella Stewart Gardner Museum—still the largest unsolved art theft in history—one of the stolen Degas paintings is delivered to the Boston studio of a young artist. Claire Roth has entered into a Faustian bargain with a powerful gallery owner by agreeing to forge the Degas in exchange for a one-woman show in his renowned gallery. But as she begins her work, she starts to suspect that this long-missing masterpiece—the very one that had been hanging at the Gardner for one hundred years—may itself be a forgery. *The Art Forger* is a thrilling novel about seeing—and not seeing—the secrets that lie beneath the canvas.

"[Shapiro] has such interesting things to say about authenticity—in both art and love—that her novel becomes not just emotionally involving but addictive." —**Entertainment Weekly**

[Shapiro] knows art history, painting techniques, and how forgers have managed through the centuries to dupe buyers into paying for fakes . . . Inventive and entertaining." —*The Boston Globe* (a *Boston Globe* **Best Crime Book of 2012**)

"[A] nimble mystery." —*The New York Times Book Review*

"If Bridget Jones's Diary and The Da Vinci Code had a love child, this would be it." —*Elle*

"An intelligent, cleverly plotted page-turner." —**Minneapolis Star Tribune**

"[A] gripping novel." —**O: The Oprah Magazine**

"Ingeniously and skillfully plotted."—*The Huffington Post*

"Engaging storytelling. Intelligent entertainment." —**Kirkus Reviews**

"Precise and exciting . . . A multi-layered narration rich with a sense of moral consequence." —*The Washington Post*

ABOUT THE AUTHOR: **B. A. Shapiro** lives in Boston and teaches fiction writing at Northeastern University.

May 2013 | Trade Paperback | Fiction | 84 pp | $14.95 | ISBN 9781616203160
Algonquin Books | workman.com | BAShapiroBooks.com

CONVERSATION STARTERS

1. At the novel's opening, Claire is a pariah in the art world. Has the community been unfair to her? In what ways, if any, is she responsible for her own exile? Does she share any blame for Isaac Cullion's death?

2. *The Art Forger* explores the darker side of human nature. All of the characters in the novel have a price, a line they're willing to cross to further their own ambitions. Do you think Claire does the wrong things for the right reasons? Is she a moral person or not? What about Isabella Stewart Gardener? What compromises would you make to secure what you most desire?

3. The novel explores the idea that we often only see what we want to see. If an expert is told a painting is a masterpiece, she sees one. If an artist desires recognition, she convinces herself that her deal with the devil is for good. How are people complicit in missing the truth?

4. Art forger Han van Meegeren, whose techniques Claire uses to create her own forgery, was a frustrated Dutch painter. An unappreciated artist struggling for recognition, his intention was to hoodwink the art dealers and critics who refused to recognize his own artistic genius. How is Claire similar to or different from Meegeren?

5. Gorgeous art can make people do incredibly ugly things, and the novel seems to suggest that it's not only for money. Why do you think that beauty and originality can have that effect on people?

6. What do the meetings between Edgar Degas and Isabella Stewart Gardner show about the relationship between a collector and an artist?

7. Claire falls hard for Aiden Markel, but she keeps secrets from him. He is also keeping secrets from her. Can a relationship survive this kind of betrayal? Do you think Aiden loves Claire? Why does Claire choose the wrong men? Do you think Aiden and Claire love art more than they love each other?

8. At the end of the novel, critics are praising Claire's work. Collectors are clamoring for the very same paintings that have hung, unsalable, in her studio for years. Why is her work suddenly more valuable? Is she successful only because she has become a celebrity?

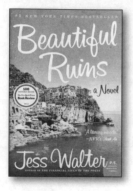

BEAUTIFUL RUINS

Jess Walter

From the moment it opens—on a rocky patch of Italian coastline, circa 1962, when a daydreaming young innkeeper looks out over the water and spies a mysterious woman approaching him on a boat—Jess Walter's *Beautiful Ruins* is a dazzling, yet deeply human, roller coaster of a novel. From the lavish set of Cleopatra to the shabby revelry of the Edinburgh Fringe Festival, to the back lots of contemporary Hollywood, *Beautiful Ruins* is gloriously inventive and constantly surprising—a story of flawed yet fascinating people navigating the rocky shores of their lives while clinging to their improbable dreams.

"Why mince words? Beautiful Ruins *is an absolute masterpiece.*" —**Richard Russo, author of** *That Old Cape Magic* **and** *Empire Falls*

"A literary miracle." —**Maureen Corrigan, NPR's** *Fresh Air*

"A high-wire feat of bravura storytelling. . . . You're going to love this book." —**Helen Schulman,** *The New York Times Book Review*

"Walter has planted himself firmly in the first rank of American authors. He has crafted a novel with pathos, piercing wit, and, most important, the generous soul of a literary classic." —**Steve Almond,** *The Boston Globe*

ABOUT THE AUTHOR: **Jess Walter** is the author of six novels, including the national bestseller *The Financial Lives of the Poets*, the National Book Award finalist *The Zero*, and *Citizen Vince*, winner of the Edgar Award for best novel. His collection of short fiction, *We Live in Water*, has just been published by Harper Perennial. He lives in Spokane, Washington.

April 2013 | Trade Paperback | Fiction | 368 pp | $15.99 | ISBN 9780061928178
Harper Perennial | harpercollins.com | www.jesswalter.com

CONVERSATION STARTERS

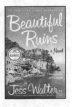

1. What does the title, *Beautiful Ruins*, refer to and how does it capture the essence of the novel?

2. At the beginning of the story, Pasquale Tursi is waiting "for life to come and find him." Is Dee Moray the "life" he was waiting for? Do you think most people wait for life—like a movie—to begin? Why?

3. When he first sees Dee, Pasquale thinks, "Life is a blatant act of imagination." Explain what he means. Do you agree with Pasquale?

4. Most of the novel's characters—Alvis Bender, Dee Moray, Shane Wheeler, Claire Silver, Pat Bender, even Richard Burton—have dreams. What are these dreams and how do they parallel and collide? How do their dreams play out in their lives? What would life be like if we didn't have dreams? What happens when they don't come true?

5. How would you characterize Michael Deane? One reviewer commented that he "has finer hidden instincts than the ones he has allowed to shape his life." When we meet him, Michael Deane seems like a parody of a Hollywood producer. What are the driving forces that propel his actions and how do they confound our expectations?

6. At the center of the novel, though largely offstage, is the legendary Hollywood production of *Cleopatra*. How is the movie symbolic of the novel's themes? How does Hollywood both fuel fantasies and destroy dreams? How is this demonstrated in the experiences of the novel's characters?

7. In Hollywood, everything happens because of the pitch. Have we become a nation of individuals pitching to each other? How would you pitch your life story to someone? How would you pitch *Beautiful Ruins*?

8. In the present day, the elderly Pasquale shares the story of his first meeting with Dee, describing it as "the moment that lasts forever." Why is this so for Pasquale? How does this revelation influence Shane and Claire? Have you ever had a moment like this?

9. How do dreams—like love—inspire us and hurt us? Do you agree with Michael's adage: *we want what we want*? Do you think this changes with age and maturity?

10. How would you describe *Beautiful Ruins*?

BETWEEN HEAVEN AND TEXAS

Marie Bostwick

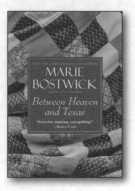

In this luminous prequel to her beloved Cobbled Court Quilts series, *New York Times* bestselling author Marie Bostwick takes readers into the heart of a small Texas town and the soul of a woman who discovers her destiny there . . .

Welcome to Too Much—where the women are strong-willed and the men are handsome yet shiftless. Ever since Mary Dell Templeton and her twin sister Lydia Dale were children, their Aunt Velvet has warned them away from local boys. But it's well known that the females in Mary Dell's family have two traits in common—superior sewing skills and a fatal weakness for men.

While Lydia Dale grows up petite and pretty, Mary Dell just keeps growing. Tall, smart, and sassy, she is determined to one day turn her love of sewing into a business. Meanwhile, she'll settle for raising babies with her new husband, Donny. But that dream proves elusive too, until finally, Mary Dell gets the son she always wanted—a child as different as he is wonderful. And as Mary Dell is forced to reconsider what truly matters in her family and her marriage, she begins to piece together a life that, like the quilts she creates, will prove vibrant, rich, and absolutely unforgettable.

"Brilliant . . . the characters thunder with life right off the page and into your heart in this quintessential story of family, forgiveness, and nobility." —**Dorothea Benton Frank,** *The New York Times* **bestselling author**

"This book wrapped around my heart with all the love, warmth, and beauty of a favorite family quilt. I can't stop thinking about it!" —**Robyn Carr, #1** *The New York Times* **bestselling author**

"So full of heart, it's amazing. Her characters feel genuine and their wisdom in the face of intense difficulty is profound." —*RT Book Reviews,* **4.5 stars, TOP PICK!**

ABOUT THE AUTHOR: **Marie Bostwick** was born and raised in the northwest. In the three decades since her marriage, Marie and her family have moved frequently, living in eight different states at eighteen different addresses, three of them in Texas.

May 2013 | Trade Paperback | Fiction | 368 pp | $15.00 | ISBN 9780758269294
Kensington Books | kensingtonbooks.com | mariebostwick.com

CONVERSATION STARTERS

1. As the story opens, Mary Dell is only minutes away from walking down the aisle, but she is having second thoughts. Why was she so hesitant to go through with the wedding? Have you been or known a bride who had second thoughts in the days or hours before a wedding ceremony? Did they or you go through with it?

2. After Howard's birth, Mary Dell's mother, Taffy, thoughtlessly uses the "R-word" in reference to her grandson and elicits a furious response from Mary Dell. How do you respond when someone uses cruel or cutting language to belittle or marginalize a person or group? If you choose to confront or have decided that you're going to in the future, what do you think is the most effective means of doing so?

3. After Donny leaves, Mary Dell sinks into depression. Silky informs her granddaughter that, upon becoming a mother, Mary Dell gave up her right to fall apart, that she has to stay strong for her child no matter what. Do you think that is true? Do you think it is fair?

4. Lydia Dale and Graydon were in love once and planned to marry. However, circumstances and miscommunication got in the way of their plans. Now that circumstances have thrown them back together again, Lydia Dale and Graydon are very different people. What has changed about them? Have you ever crossed paths with an old boyfriend or girlfriend after a space of years? What kinds of feelings did that bring forth?

5. Aunt Velvet makes much of the Tudmore family's "Fatal Flaw," a tendency for the women of the line to lose their normally solid good sense in the presence of a certain sort of man. Just for fun: What kind of man makes you go weak in the knees?

6. As a little girl, Mary Dell dreamed of owning her own dress shop in downtown Too Much. Her dream faded with the passage of time, almost forgotten until she stumbles upon an unexpected opportunity to resurrect it, albeit in a different form, by buying a quilt shop. How about you? Do you have a dream that you've let fade? Discuss the fears and obstacles that have impeded you; brainstorm about ways to overcome them.

BLUE ASYLUM

Kathy Hepinstall

Amid the mayhem of the Civil War, Iris Dunleavy is put on trial by her husband, convicted of madness, and sent to Sanibel Asylum to be restored to a compliant Virginia plantation wife. But her husband is the true criminal; she is no lunatic, only guilty of disagreeing on notions of cruelty and property.

On this remote Florida island, Iris meets a wonderful collection of inmates in various states of sanity, including Ambrose Weller, a Confederate soldier haunted by war, whose dark eyes beckon to Iris. Can such love be real? And if they do find a way out, will there be any way—any place—for them to make a life together?

"An absorbing story that explores both the rewards and perils of love, pride, and sanity" (*Publishers Weekly*), *Blue Asylum* is a beautiful tale of impossible love and the undeniable call of freedom.

"*[A] lush, brainy Southern gothic novel. . . . Hepinstall makes inspired use of the Civil War as a means to explore notions of freedom, courage and, especially, opposing principles that both prevent and create change.*" —**Atlanta Journal Constitution**

"Blue Asylum *casts a spell that keeps the reader turning pages as if in a trance. The language is lyrical but the plot is taut and compelling. Kathy Hepinstall is a master storyteller in full command of her craft.*" —**Elizabeth Forsythe Hailey, author of the beloved bestseller A Woman of Independent Means**

"*A first-rate choice for fans of intelligent historical romances.*" —**Library Journal, starred**

About the Author: **Kathy Hepinstall** is the author of three previous novels, *The House of Gentle Men* (a *Los Angeles Times* bestseller), *The Absence of Nectar* (a national bestseller), and *The Prince of Lost Places*. She is an award-winning creative director and advertising writer, whose clients have included top brands in American business. She grew up in Texas.

April 2013 | Trade Paperback | Fiction | 288 pp | $14.95 | ISBN 9780544002227
Houghton Mifflin Harcourt | hmhbooks.com | kathyhepinstall.com

CONVERSATION STARTERS

1. When you first meet Iris, Wendell, and Ambrose in chapter 1, do they seem mad to you? How do they see one another, and how true do you think their first impressions turn out to be? Use examples from the novel to support your opinion.

2. Do you think Iris had any influence over whether Ambrose lived or died? What lessons do you think she learned by the end of the story?

3. Describe Dr. Cowell's criteria for a "sane" wife. Then, compare Dr. Cowell's relationship with his wife, Mary, to what the doctor tells his women patients they should be to their husbands

4. In what ways does Wendell identify with the inmates at Sanibel? How does he set himself apart from them?

5. Discuss Dr. Cowell's relationship with his wife and child, and also with the inmates collectively. Do you think the Cowells love each other? Do you think Dr. Cowell loves his work more or less than his family, and why? Use examples from the novel to justify your opinion.

6. When Iris first asks Wendell to help her escape from the island, he hesitates. With what is he struggling? Why does he first refuse to help Iris and Ambrose? Do you think he's right, or is it like Iris says, that he's "just like his father"?

7. Dr. Cowell changes his mind about Iris several times throughout the novel. What prompts him to consider for the first time that Iris might be telling the truth—that she is the victim of her husband's lies and base character? What changes his mind again?

8. This novel takes a look at the effects of betrayal on multiple levels. Identify each instance of betrayal in the novel and discuss each character's motivations. Do you feel anyone is 100% justified in their actions? Why or why not?

9. Discuss the ending of the novel. Why do you think the author chose to end with Dr. Cowell back at the asylum, waiting for the mad old woman to come in for her appointment, and with the image of the woman dancing on the beach with her imagined husband? What is the significance of the birds' perspective of the scene?

BODIES OF WATER

T. Greenwood

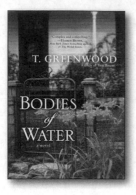

In 1960, Billie Valentine is a young housewife living in a sleepy Massachusetts suburb, treading water in a dull marriage and caring for two adopted daughters. Summers spent with the girls at their lakeside camp in Vermont are her one escape—from her husband's demands, from days consumed by household drudgery, and from the nagging suspicion that life was supposed to hold something different.

Then a new family moves in across the street. Ted and Eva Wilson have three children and a fourth on the way, and their arrival reignites long-buried feelings in Billie. The affair that follows offers a solace Billie has never known, until her secret is revealed and both families are wrenched apart in the tragic aftermath.

Fifty years later, Ted and Eva's son, Johnny, contacts an elderly but still spry Billie, entreating her to return east to meet with him. Once there, Billie finally learns the surprising truth about what was lost, and what still remains, of those joyful, momentous summers.

In this deeply tender novel, T. Greenwood weaves deftly between the past and present to create a poignant and wonderfully moving story of friendship, the resonance of memories, and the love that keeps us afloat.

"Complex and compelling."—**Eleanor Brown**, *The New York Times* **bestselling author of** *The Weird Sisters*

ABOUT THE AUTHOR: **T. Greenwood** is the author of seven novels, including *Two Rivers* and *The Hungry Season*. She has received numerous grants for her writing, including a National Endowment for the Arts Literature Fellowship and a grant from the Maryland State Arts Council. She lives in San Diego, California, with her husband and their two daughters where she teaches creative writing, studies photography, and continues to write.

October 2013 | Trade Paperback | Fiction | 384 pp | $15.00 | ISBN 9780758250933
Kensington Books | kensingtonbooks.com | tgreenwood.com

CONVERSATION STARTERS

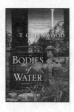

1. This is a love story, but it is also the story of an infidelity. Discuss how that impacts your reading of the characters and empathy to their situations.

2. Billie's insecurities about herself as a mother run deep. Are they warranted? Is she a good mother? Why or why not?

3. What does Eva represent to Billie? Do you think Eva was in love with her specifically or with the notion of her? Do you think she would have stayed with Billie had she made it to Vermont?

4. Each woman has a different motive for getting involved in this relationship. What are these motives? What does each woman gain from the other's love and companionship?

5. Billie has made a life for herself in California. Do you think she is truly happy? How about at the end of the novel, once she knows what really happened to Eva?

6. Discuss each of the marriages (Ted and Eva, Billie and Frankie). How would you characterize these men? How are they similar? How are they different?

7. What do you think motivates Johnny to orchestrate the reunion between Eva and Billie?

8. What does Billie sacrifice in order to move on with her life? Are there any other victims here?

9. Do you think that Gussy knew what was transpiring between Eva and Billie? Was she complicit in the affair? Do you think she knew that Eva survived the crash? If so, why would she not tell Billie?

10. In the end, Johnny tells Billie that Ted lied to end the affair, and told Frankie that Billie was dead. Do you think Frankie would have told Billie the truth if he knew it?

11. How might the love story between Billie and Eva played out if they had met in 2013 instead of the 1960s?

12. Reread the opening paragraphs to the first and last chapters. Has the concept of memory evolved over the course of the novel? If so, how? If not, discuss the consistencies. Talk about the importance of memory in the book and in the way you experience your own lives and loves.

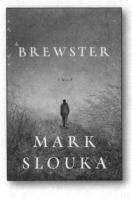

BREWSTER

Mark Slouka

A powerful story about an unforgettable friendship between two teenage boys and their hopes for escape from a dead-end town.

The year is 1968. The world is changing, and sixteen-year-old Jon Mosher is determined to change with it. Racked by guilt over his older brother's childhood death and stuck in the dead-end town of Brewster, New York, he turns his rage into victories running track. Meanwhile, Ray Cappicciano, a rebel as gifted with his fists as Jon is with his feet, is trying to take care of his baby brother while staying out of the way of his abusive, ex-cop father. When Jon and Ray form a tight friendship, they find in each other everything they lack at home, but it's not until Ray falls in love with beautiful, headstrong Karen Dorsey that the three friends begin to dream of breaking away from Brewster for good. Freedom, however, has its price. As forces beyond their control begin to bear down on them, Jon sets off on the race of his life—a race to redeem his past and save them all.

Mark Slouka's work has been called "relentlessly observant, miraculously expressive" (*The New York Times Book Review*). Reverberating with compassion, heartache, and grace, *Brewster* is an unforgettable coming-of-age story from one of our most compelling novelists.

"*The dark undertow of Slouka's prose makes* Brewster *instantly mesmerizing, a novel that whirls the reader into small-town, late 1960s America with mastery, originality, and heart.*" —**Jennifer Egan, Pulitzer Prize winning author of *A Visit from the Goon Squad***

ABOUT THE AUTHOR: **Mark Slouka** is the author of four previous works of fiction including *Lost Lake*, a *New York Times* Notable Book, and *The Visible World*, a finalist for the British Book Award. His 2011 essay collection, "Essays from the Nick of Time," was the winner of the PEN/Diamonstein-Speilvogel Award. He lives in Brewster, New York.

August 2013 | Hardcover | Fiction | 288 pp | $25.95 | ISBN 9780393239751
W. W. Norton & Company | wwnorton.com
Sign up for the Norton newsletter & giveaways: http://bit.ly/wwnorton-reading-group-guides

CONVERSATION STARTERS

1. The novel is named for the town it is set in, and it has a tremendously vivid sense of place. Describe the town of Brewster. In what ways is the setting important to this novel?

2. Jon's affair with Tina feels like a hiatus, a brief escape from his real life and troubles, and she never reappears in the story. What might Jon have learned from his relationship with Tina that he brings to the rest of his experiences in the novel?

3. Discuss the character of Karen Dorsey. What draws Ray and Jon to her, and she to them? What do you think made Karen choose Ray over Jon? If you were Karen, whom would you prefer?

4. Who's your favorite adult character in *Brewster*? Falvo? Jimmy? Mr. Mosher? Someone else? Why?

5. *Brewster* can be characterized as a coming-of-age story. Describe the ways in which Jon, Ray, and Karen grow over the course of the novel. What do they each learn about themselves, the nature of love, and the wider world?

6. Describe how the novel treats first love. Did it feel real to you or remind you of the first time you fell in love?

7. Jon's parents and Ray's father all have dark pasts, and both families are abusive, though the abuse takes different forms. Are there parallels to be drawn between Jon and Ray's families? Jon and Ray each find some acceptance with the other's family. Discuss how this happened and why it makes sense.

8. What does running come to mean to Jon? Does it mean something different at the beginning of the novel than it does at the end?

9. In the final chapter, Jon says, "I thought about him over the years. Wondered, sometimes, if it could have all played differently. If we'd lost, maybe, before we started." Discuss the ending of the novel. Do you think that Jon, Ray, and Karen were doomed from the start? In what ways will the characters escape Brewster, and in what ways will it never truly leave them? Do you feel that your own hometown has left an imprint on you?

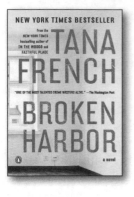

BROKEN HARBOR

Tana French

The latest *New York Times* bestseller from the acclaimed author of *In the Woods* and *Faithful Place*

Tana French's rise can only be called meteoric. Starting with her award-winning debut, French has scored four consecutive *The New York Times* bestsellers and established herself as one of the top names in the genre. *Broken Harbor* is quintessential French—a damaged hero, an unspeakable crime, and an intricately plotted mystery—nestled in a timely examination of lives shattered by the global economic downturn.

Mick "Scorcher" Kennedy always brings in the killer. Always. That's why he's landed this high-profile triple homicide. At first, he thinks it's going to be simple, but the murder scene holds terrifying memories for Scorcher. Memories of something that happened there back when he was a boy.

"One of the most talented crime writers alive." —**The Washington Post**

"Ms. French created haunting, damaged characters who have been hit hard by some cataclysm . . . This may sound like a routine police procedural. But like Gillian Flynn's Gone Girl, *this summer's other dagger-sharp display of mind games,* Broken Harbor *is something more."* —**Janet Maslin, The New York Times**

"So much of the pleasure inherent in reading these novels is in trying to figure out where things are going and being constantly surprised, not to mention thoroughly spooked. I predict Broken Harbor *will be on more than one Best of 2012 lists—it's definitely at the top of mine."* —**The Associated Press**

*"*Broken Harbor *is truly a book for, and of, our broken times. It's literature masquerading as a police procedural."* —**The Cleveland Plain Dealer**

ABOUT THE AUTHOR: **Tana French** grew up in Ireland, Italy, the U.S. and Malawi, and has lived in Dublin since 1990. She trained as a professional actress at Trinity College, Dublin, and has worked in theatre, film, and voiceover.

April 2013 | Trade Paperback | Fiction | 464 pp | $16.00 | ISBN 9780143123309
Penguin Books | us.penguinbooks.com | tanafrench.com

CONVERSATION STARTERS

1. French's protagonist, Mick "Scorcher" Kennedy, prides himself on his self-control. Is Scorcher's self-control as strong as he imagines? In what other ways might Scorcher's self-image be somewhat incorrect?

2. French writes with considerable affection for Ireland. However, her books often contain more than a hint of lament for the country's recent decline. What aspects of Ireland in the present day seem to sadden her most?

3. Scorcher believes that post-modern society has begun to turn "feral" and that "everything that stops us being animals is eroding, washing away like sand." Do you agree with Scorcher's assessment? Explain why or why not. How does Scorcher's view of society dovetail with his self-image?

4. How do Scorcher's class prejudices affect his perceptions of the Spain case? Is class bias the only reason he is so desperate to believe in the integrity of Patrick Spain?

5. The relationship between Scorcher and Richie evolves rapidly, beginning as one between an all-wise mentor and his trainee but transforming into a much more contentious one. Discuss this evolution and the ways French uses it to develop the two men's characters.

6. Why do *you* think Scorcher doesn't want to have children? Try to come up with as many plausible explanations as you can.

7. Tana French is a master of creating characters with virtues that are turned into vices by unlucky circumstances. What are some examples of this kind of characterization in *Broken Harbor*, and how do they act as a commentary on human nature?

8. Explaining her madness, Dina says, "There is no why." Why is this statement especially disturbing to her brother, Scorcher?

9. How has Scorcher's childhood shaped the person he is now?

10. How have the more youthful experiences of Conor, Pat, and Jenny shaped their characters and destinies?

11. Tana French manages the emotions of her interrogation scenes with great expertise, creating tremendous tensions and moving toward great crescendos of feeling. Read over one of these scenes and discuss how the emotional force builds, breaks, and subsides.

CARISSIMA

Rosanna Chiofalo

From Rosanna Chiofalo comes a sumptuous new novel that sweeps readers from the Italian-American enclave of Astoria, New York, to the stunning vistas of Rome, and introduces two very different women—in a story of friendship, love, and destiny…

In college, Pia Santore dreamed of going to New York and taking the Big Apple by storm with her younger sister Erica. Instead, Pia has arrived in Astoria, Queens, with a prestigious journalism internship at a celebrity magazine . . . and without Erica. Though the neighborhood has an abundance of appeal—including the delectable confections sold at her Aunt Antoniella's bakery—the pain of losing Erica a few years ago still feels fresh.

Pia's arrival coincides with an unexpected sighting. Italian movie icon Francesca Donata is rumored to be staying nearby, every bit as voluptuous and divaesque as in her heyday. With the help of a handsome local artist with ties to Francesca's family, Pia convinces the legend to grant her a series of interviews—even traveling to her house in Rome. In the eternal city, Pia begins to unearth the truth behind the star's fabled romances and tangled past. And here too, where beauty and history mingle in every breathtaking view, and hope shimmers in the Trevi fountain and on the Spanish Steps, Pia gradually learns how to love and when to let go. For when in Rome, you may find your carissima—your dearest one—and you may even find yourself.

"Fantastico! I couldn't put it down!"—**Lisa Jackson, #1** *New York Times* **bestselling author**

ABOUT THE AUTHOR: **Rosanna Chiofalo** is a first-generation Italian American whose parents emigrated from Sicily to New York in the early 1960s. After graduating with a BA in English from Stony Brook University, Rosanna knew she wanted to be around books and have a career in writing. For twenty years, she's worked as a Copywriter and Copy Director for several New York City publishing houses.

September 2013 | Trade Paperback | Fiction | 464 pp | $15.00 | ISBN 9780758275042
Kensington Books | kensingtonbooks.com | rosannachiofalo.com

CONVERSATION STARTERS

1. Why do you think Francesca is obsessed with being adored by her public? Why do you think the neighbors in Astoria are so fascinated by Francesca, besides the obvious reason of her being a star?

2. Do you think Signora Tesca was justified in holding a grudge against Francesca for all those years? How much do you think jealousy played a part in her refusal to talk to Francesca for so long?

3. How was Pia's relationship with her late sister Erica different than Francesca's relationship with her sister? How have both of these women been influenced by their sisters?

4. Compare and contrast Pia and Francesca. How are their dreams and goals similar? How are they different?

5. We first meet Signora Tesca in *Bella Fortuna*. What were your first impressions of her in *Bella Fortuna*? Did your impressions change when you encountered her again in *Carissima*? If so, how? The same question for Antoniella. How have your initial impressions about her changed from the first book to this one?

6. Francesca is infatuated with jewelry almost as much as she is with being loved by her fans. Why do you think she loves jewelry so much? Of the gifts that Rocco gives her, which was your favorite?

7. Do you feel that Gregory's sudden discovery as an artist goes to his head? Why do you think many people become more self-absorbed when they find fame and/or success in their lives?

8. Do you feel sorry for Francesca in the beginning of the novel when you learn that her five engagements never resulted in marriage? How has her decision to remain single shaped the person she's become? Do you feel sorry for her toward the end of the novel? Do you think she's grown?

9. Francesca chooses to wear *il lutto,* the dress for mourning, after her sister dies. This custom has been losing popularity in Italy over the years. What do you think of it? Were you surprised that a glamorous star like Francesca chose to honor this decades-old Italian custom?

10. How has Pia's trip to Rome changed her? Do you think she would have had the same insights if she had not gone to Rome?

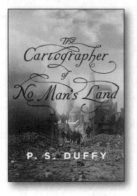

THE CARTOGRAPHER OF NO MAN'S LAND

P. S. Duffy

From a hardscrabble village in Nova Scotia to the collapsing trenches of France, a debut novel about a family divided by World War I.

In the tradition of Robert Goolrick's *A Reliable Wife* and Karl Marlantes's *Matterhorn*, P. S. Duffy's astonishing debut showcases a rare and instinctive talent emerging in midlife. Her novel leaps across the Atlantic, between a father at war and a son coming of age at home without him.

When his beloved brother-in-law goes missing at the front in 1916, Angus defies his pacifist upbringing to join the war and find him. Assured a position as a cartographer in London, he is instead sent directly into the visceral shock of battle. Meanwhile, at home, his son Simon Peter must navigate escalating hostility in a fishing village torn by grief. With the intimacy of *The Song of Achilles* and the epic scope of *The Invisible Bridge*, *The Cartographer of No Man's Land* offers a soulful portrayal of World War I and the lives that were forever changed by it, both on the battlefield and at home.

"Brilliant. The description of front line action in the trenches is impressively real, and the ending blessedly free from sentimentality. Altogether a remarkable debut." —**Simon Mawer, author of *Trapeze* and *The Glass Room***

"Cutting deftly between a father at war and a son at home, The Cartographer of No Man's Land *is a graceful, dignified look at all the ways in which war is endured: from the stories people tell to keep themselves alive at the front, to the fault lines that threaten the home-front bond. This is a moving and memorable debut."* —**Jessica Francis Kane, author of *The Report***

ABOUT THE AUTHOR: **P. S. Duffy** traces her Nova Scotian roots back over 250 years. She herself sailed in Mahone Bay, Nova Scotia, for thirty summers. She now lives with her husband in Rochester, Minnesota. This is her first novel.

October 2013 | Hardcover | Fiction | 384 pp | $25.95 | ISBN 9780871403766
Liveright | wwnorton.com | psduffy.com
Sign up for the Norton newsletter & giveaways: http://bit.ly/wwnorton-reading-group-guides

1. In the beginning of the novel, Colonel Chisholm relays to Angus that he was selected to take on the role of first lieutenant due to his education and maturity. Do you think these characteristics accurately describe Angus? What other qualities prepared him for this role?

2. Why do you think Angus chooses not to tell Hettie that he found Ebbin? How would the truth affect Hettie? How does the secret change Angus and Hettie's marriage?

3. Birds are a recurring motif in the novel: the lark nesting in a German jacket, the drawing Angus makes for Paul of a lark, etc. What is the impact of these repeated images?

4. Why does the town begin to turn on Avon Heist? Do you think he could have prevented his arrest? Are there other examples of the war bringing out unexpected behavior in characters in the novel?

5. Why does Ebbin take on the identity of Havers? In the moment of Ebbin's death, he calls Angus by his name. Do you think that Ebbin knows who Angus is throughout his time as Havers, or is Ebbin's identity as Havers all-encompassing until he is faced with death?

6. What role do Juliette and Paul play in Angus's recovery? What do they do for him, and what does he mean to them?

7. How does the prologue of the father and son at sea frame the novel?

8. Were you surprised when Angus learned that Conlon had taken his own life? What about Conlon's character may have led him to succumb?

9. Why does Simon want to name the boat he helped design with Philip *"True North"*? Is there more than one meaning behind the name?

10. Escape is one of many themes in the book. Identify several instances that exemplify the theme of escape. Is physical escape different from emotional escape?

11. When Simon and Duncan examine Angus's painting of the father and son on a boat, it quickly becomes apparent that the identities of the father and son are ambiguous. Who do you think Angus is portraying in the picture? Is it possible that there is not a concrete answer?

THE CHAPERONE
Laura Moriarty

Only a few years before becoming a famous silent-film star and an icon of her generation, a fifteen-year-old Louise Brooks leaves Wichita, Kansas, to study with the prestigious Denishawn School of Dancing in New York. Much to her annoyance, she is accompanied by a thirty-six-year-old chaperone, who is neither mother nor friend. Cora Carlisle, a complicated but traditional woman with her own reasons for making the trip, has no idea what she's in for. Young Louise, already stunningly beautiful and sporting her famous black bob with blunt bangs, is known for her arrogance and her lack of respect for convention. Ultimately, the five weeks they spend together will transform their lives forever.

For Cora, the city holds the promise of discovery that might answer the question at the core of her being, and even as she does her best to watch over Louise in this strange and bustling place she embarks on a mission of her own. And while what she finds isn't what she anticipated, she is liberated in a way she could not have imagined. Over the course of Cora's relationship with Louise, her eyes are opened to the promise of the twentieth century and a new understanding of the possibilities for being fully alive.

"Enthralling." —*O, The Oprah Magazine*

"Captivating and wise . . . [An] inventive and lovely Jazz Age story." —*The Washington Post*

ABOUT THE AUTHOR: **Laura Moriarty** earned a degree in social work before returning for her M.A. in Creative Writing at the University of Kansas. She was the recipient of the George Bennett Fellowship for Creative Writing at Phillips Exeter Academy in New Hampshire. She lives with her daughter in Lawrence, Kansas.

June 2013 | Trade Paperback | Fiction | 416 pp | $16.00 | ISBN 9781594631436
Riverhead | us.penguingroup.com | lauramoriarty.net

CONVERSATION STARTERS

1. *The Chaperone* opens with Cora Carlisle waiting out a rainstorm in a car with a friend when she hears about Louise Brooks for the first time. What do we learn about Cora in this scene? What does it tell us about her and the world she lives in? Why does Laura Moriarty, the author, choose to open the novel this way? Why do you think she waits to introduce us to Brooks?

2. When Cora arrives in New York, the city is worlds away from her life in Wichita. How much do you think Cora actually embraces New York? When she returns to Wichita, what does she bring back with her from New York? What parts of her stayed true to Wichita all along?

3. The limits of acceptable behavior for women were rapidly changing in the 1920s, and both Cora Carlisle and Louise Brooks, in their own ways, push against these boundaries. Discuss the different ways the two women try to change society's expectations for women. Is one more successful than the other? What are the values involved in each woman's approach?

4. Cora becomes frustrated with the hypocrisy of the women in her Wichita circle of friends and yet she herself chooses to keep details about her own life secret. Do you think she should be more open about her life choices? What are the risks for her if she were to be more open?

5. Cora Carlisle hopes to find the secret of her past in New York City but discovers that the truth doesn't align with either her expectations or her memory of the past. Why do you think Laura Moriarty has chosen to leave Cora's history ambiguous? What does this tell you about Cora? How has Cora's attitude toward her past changed by the end of *The Chaperone*?

6. Cora narrates the events of the book from a perspective of many years later. What juxtapositions does this allow her? By placing Cora's narration at a time of radical social change, what parallels is Moriarty making?

7. Think about Louise Brooks's behavior. How much of it would be considered scandalous today? What values has society held on to? In what ways has society changed?

THE CHERRY COLA BOOK CLUB

Ashton Lee

With its corrugated iron siding and cramped interior, the Cherico, Mississippi, library is no Antebellum gem. But for young librarian Maura Beth Mayhew, it's as essential to the community as the delicious desserts at the Twinkle, Twinkle Café. It's a place for neighbors to mingle and browse through the newest bestsellers, for the indomitable Miss Voncille Nettles to host her "Who's Who in Cherico?" meetings. The library may be underfunded and overlooked, but it's Maura Beth's pride, and she won't let the good ol' boys on the City Council close it down without a fight.

Which is why Maura Beth has founded the Cherry Cola Book Club—a last-ditch attempt to boost circulation and save her job. Over potluck dinners featuring treasured family recipes, the booklovers of Cherico come together to talk about literary classics. But soon it's not just Margaret Mitchell and Harper Lee being discussed over chicken gumbo and home-made biscuits with green pepper jelly. Secrets are shared, old dreams rekindled, and new loves slowly blossom.

Southern charm, wit, and warmth combine in this delightful novel about great books, true friends, and the stories that give life its richest meaning, on and off the page.

"For anyone who has ever believed in the power of a good book, Ashton Lee's charming novel of a small Southern town with a flavorful plan to save its precious but woefully underfunded library will have you cheering from the start. Clever, sassy, and as tasty as an icebox pie, The Cherry Cola Book Club *is a rare treat. Community activism has never been more delicious— or more fun."* —**Erika Marks, author of** *Little Gale Gumbo* **and** *The Mermaid Collector*

ABOUT THE AUTHOR: **Ashton Lee** is from Oxford, Mississippi, but was born in historic Natchez. He comes from a large Southern family, which provides fodder for his fiction.

April 2013 | Trade Paperback | Fiction | 272 pp | $15.00 | ISBN 9780758273413
Kensington Books | kensingtonbooks.com

CONVERSATION STARTERS

1. Discuss the female character that fascinates you the most and give the pros and cons of her personality.

2. Discuss the male character that fascinates you the most and give the pros and cons of his personality.

3. Assign someone to argue for the Cherico Library's existence against someone else who supports the City Council's point of view for its dissolution. Let the group decide who won the argument.

4. Does Cherico reflect some of the economic and cultural realities of your home town?

5. Which of the couples most resembles your relationship with your spouse or significant other? (Becca and Stout Fella, Miss Voncille and Locke Linwood, Douglas and Connie)

6. The character of Pamela Linwood, though deceased, plays an important role in the plot. How do each of you view that role?

7. What has your local library meant to you?

8. Over the long haul, do you think Maura Beth Mayhew is fighting a losing battle?

9. Do you think taxpayers in general have a realistic view of what it takes to keep a library up and running?

10. Do you think library services should fall into the same category for funding as firefighting, police protection, streets, water, and utilities?

11. Did you ever make the sort of wish/bucket list that Maura Beth Mayhew made on page 25 of her journal (Three Things To Accomplish Before I'm Thirty)?

12. Pretend you are a female member of the Cherry Cola Book Club. Do you fall into the Scarlett or the Melanie category as a modern woman?

13. Pretend you are a member (either gender) of the Cherry Cola Book Club. What role do you think *To Kill A Mockingbird* played in the passage of 1964 Civil Rights Act, if any?

14. There will be a sequel to *The Cherry Cola Book Club*. What do you hope will happen in that book?

15. What is your favorite sequence in *The Cherry Cola Book Club*?

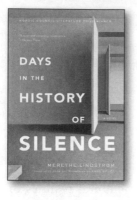

DAYS IN THE HISTORY OF SILENCE

Merethe Lindstrøm

From the acclaimed Nordic Council Literature Prize winner, a story that reveals the devastating effects of mistaking silence for peace and feeling shame for inevitable circumstances

Eva and Simon have spent most of their adult lives together. He is a physician and she is a teacher, and they have three grown daughters and a comfortable home. What binds them together isn't only affection and solidarity but also the painful facts of their respective histories, which they keep hidden even from their own children. But after the abrupt dismissal of their housekeeper and Simon's increasing withdrawal into himself, the past can no longer be repressed. Lindstrøm has crafted a masterpiece about the grave mistakes we make when we misjudge the legacy of war, common prejudices, and our own strategies of survival.

"A quiet and unnerving masterpiece." —**Norway Times**

ABOUT THE AUTHOR: **Merethe Lindstrøm** has published several collections of short stories, novels, and a children's book. She was nominated for the Nordic Council Literature Prize and the Norwegian Critics' Prize for her short-story collection *The Guests*. In 2008 she received the Dobloug Prize for her entire literary work. *Days in the History of Silence* is her most recent novel, winner of the Nordic Council Literature Prize and the Norwegian Critics' Prize for Literature, and nominated for the P2 Listeners' Novel Prize and the Youth Critics' Prize. She lives in Oslo, Norway.

August 2013 | Trade Paperback | Fiction | 240 pp | $14.95 | ISBN 9781590515952
Other Press | otherpress.com

CONVERSATION STARTERS

1. The "intruder" who enters Eva and Simon's house in the beginning of the novel is at first an unsettling presence, but later in the book he comes to represent something else to Eva. Why does Lindstrøm open with this scene, and how does it relate to the rest of the book?

2. Despite Marija's hateful anti-Semitic remarks, Eva finds herself extremely affected by her absence after she and Simon dismiss her. What role does Marija play in Simon and Eva's relationship that becomes such a profound loss after she is gone?

3. Simon and Eva both decide at different times that it's best not to tell their daughters about their respective pasts. To what extent can hiding the past from the next generation be a selfish act or a benevolent one? Is keeping painful secrets from loved ones, as Simon and Eva do throughout this novel, ever justified?

4. How do you interpret Simon's descent into silence? Is it a kind of protest, a result of dementia, or perhaps something else? Do you think Simon is making a choice to be silent? If so, why do you think he chooses silence over telling?

5. What role does guilt play in Simon and Eva's relationship with each other and with their family?

6. Simon searches for his missing relatives and Eva begins to imagine her son's fate more and more as the book progresses. How are Simon's and Eva's "searches" for missing relatives different, and how might this account for their growing distance from each other?

7. At the end of the novel, it is implied that Eva has finally decided to share the truth with her daughters. What ultimately prompts this decision? Do you feel that it is for the best?

DREAM WITH LITTLE ANGELS

Michael Hiebert

Abe Teal wasn't even born when Ruby Mae Vickers went missing twelve years ago. Few people in Alvin, Alabama, talk about the months spent looking for her, or about how Ruby Mae's lifeless body was finally found beneath a willow tree. Even Abe's mom, Leah, Alvin's only detective, has avoided the subject. But now, another girl is missing. Fourteen-year-old Mary Ann Dailey took the bus home from school as usual, then simply vanished. Townsfolk comb the dense forests and swampy creeks to no avail. Days later, Tiffany Michelle Yates disappears. Abe saw her only hours before, holding an ice cream cone and wearing a pink dress. Observant and smart, Abe watches his mother battle small-town bureaucracy and old resentments, desperate to find both girls and quietly frantic for her own children's safety. As the search takes on a terrifying urgency, Abe traverses the shifting ground between innocence and hard-won understanding, eager to know and yet fearing what will be revealed.

"One of the best books I've read in a long, long while." —**Lisa Jackson,** *The New York Times* **bestselling author**

"In Hiebert's sure hands, psychological insight and restrained lyricism combine to create a coming-of-age tale as devastating as it is indelible." —**Publishers Weekly**

"Hiebert has an authentic Southern voice and his protagonist, eleven-year-old Abe Teal, is as engaging as Harper Lee's Scout. Dream with Little Angels is a masterful coming-of-age gem." —**Deborah Crombie,** *The New York Times* **bestselling author**

ABOUT THE AUTHOR: **Michael Hiebert** likes to write surprising stories that cross genres, and are often mysterious. He is a two-time winner of the prestigious Surrey International Writer's Conference Storyteller's Award and has been listed in *The Best American Mystery Stories*, edited by Joyce Carol Oates. Michael lives in Canada with his family, a dog named Chloe, and enough books that it is no longer fun to move.

July 2013 | Trade Paperback | Fiction | 304 pp | $15.00 | ISBN 9780758285751
Kensington Books | kensingtonbooks.com | michaelhiebert.com

CONVERSATION STARTERS

1. Describe Abe's relationship with his mother. Contrast this with his relationship to his sister, Carry, especially at the beginning of the book.

2. Do you feel Leah treats Caroline differently from how she treats Abe? If so, how? How much of this difference do you think comes from Leah's own past and how much stems from Carry's newly found insolence?

3. When the boys go hunting for Mary Ann Dailey, they wind up in the woods with Mr. Garner. He tells them about Ruby Mae Vickers disappearing twelve years ago. He even goes so far as to say, "Oh, she turned up, eventually. Just not in the same state she disappeared in." Do you think this is an inappropriate conversation for him to have with eleven-year-old Abe and Dewey?

4. Other than telling the boys he put them there, Mr. Garner doesn't say much else about the fresh flowers the boys see scattered around the base of the willow where Ruby Mae Vickers's body was found. Why do you think this is?

5. Once Mary Ann Dailey hasn't shown up for several days, Leah gets paranoid for her own children's safety, to the point of not letting Abe walk with Dewey to school or allowing Caroline to walk to the bus stop. Do you think her paranoia is ungrounded, or is she acting in a rational way?

6. Where do you think Abe's constant racial statements and slurs ultimately stem from? Is he being influenced by someone or something external, or is it simply a case of innocent ignorance?

7. After solving the case, Leah takes Abe up to Cornflower Lake, where she tells him she "has to get rid of something." Carefully, she lifts the Virgin Mother from her neck. Throughout the book, Leah's played with this necklace at various times. When Abe asks her what she's going to do with it, she tells him she doesn't need it anymore and tosses it into the lake. Why does Leah do this? Why is the necklace symbolic? What part of her has been "repaired" through solving this case that's allowed her to let go of this necklace? What event had left that part in need of repairing up until now?

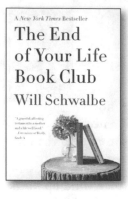

A *New York Times* Bestseller

The End of Your Life Book Club

Will Schwalbe

"A graceful, affecting testament to a mother and a life well lived." *Entertainment Weekly*, Grade A

THE END OF YOUR LIFE BOOK CLUB

Will Schwalbe

An *Entertainment Weekly* and *BookPage* Best Book of the Year

During her treatment for cancer, Mary Anne Schwalbe and her son Will spent many hours sitting in waiting rooms together. To pass the time, they would talk about the books they were reading. Once, by chance, they read the same book at the same time—and an informal book club of two was born. Through their wide-ranging reading, Will and Mary Anne—and we, their fellow readers—are reminded how books can be comforting, astonishing, and illuminating, changing the way that we feel about and interact with the world around us. A profoundly moving memoir of caregiving, mourning, and love—*The End of Your Life Book Club* is also about the joy of reading, and the ways that joy is multiplied when we share it with others.

"A graceful, affecting testament to a mother and a life well lived."
—*Entertainment Weekly*

"Schwalbe . . . highlights not just how relevant but how integral literature can be to life." —The Washington Post

"[This] book is robust with love and laughter." —Chicago Tribune

ABOUT THE AUTHOR: **Will Schwalbe** has worked in publishing (most recently as senior vice president and editor in chief of Hyperion Books); digital media, as the founder and CEO of Cookstr.com; and as a journalist, writing for various publications including *The New York Times* and the *South China Morning Post*. He is on the boards of Yale University Press and the Kingsborough Community College Foundation. He is the co-author, with David Shipley, of *Send: Why People Email So Badly and How to Do It Better*.

June 2013 | Trade Paperback | Memoir | 352 pp | $15.00 | ISBN 9780307739780
Vintage | www.randomhouse.com | theendofyourlifebookclub.com

CONVERSATION STARTERS

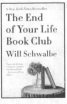

The End of Your Life Book Club
Will Schwalbe

1. Does this book have a central theme? What is it?

2. Why does Mary Anne always read a book's ending first? How does this reflect her character?

3. Early in the book, Will writes, "I wanted to learn more about my mother's life and the choices she'd made, so I often steered the conversation there. She had an agenda of her own, as she almost always did. It took me some time, and some help, to figure it out." What was Mary Anne's agenda?

4. Mary Anne underlined a passage in *Seventy Verses on Emptiness*, which resonated with Will: "Permanent is not; impermanent is not; a self is not; not a self [is not]; clean is not; not clean is not; happy is not; suffering is not." Why did this strike both of them as significant? What do you think it means?

5. Throughout the book, Will talks about books as symbols and sources of hope. How has reading books served a similar function for you?

6. How does religious belief help Mary Anne? How do you think it might have helped Will?

7. Will is amazed by his mother's ability to continue her efforts to fund the library in Afghanistan even while facing a death sentence, until he realizes that "she used her emotions to motivate her and help her concentrate. The emphasis for her was always on doing what needed to be done. I had to learn this lesson while she was still there to teach me." Did Will learn? What makes you think so?

8. Why did Mary Anne become so intent on certain things happening—Obama's election, David Rohde's safe return? Will talks about his own "magical thinking" several times in the book—what form do you think Mary Anne's took?

9. "We're all in the end-of-our-life book club, whether we acknowledge it or not; each book we read may well be the last, each conversation the final one." How did this realization affect Will's final days with his mom?

10. Which of the books discussed by Will and Mary Anne have you read? Which do you most want to read?

EQUILIBRIUM

Lorrie Thomson

In the year since her husband died, Laura Klein's world has shifted on its axis. It's not just that she's raising two children alone—fact is, Laura always did the parenting for both of them. But now her fifteen-year-old daughter, Darcy, is dating a boy with a fast car and faster hands, and thirteen-year-old Troy's attitude has plummeted along with his voice. Just when she's resigning herself to a life of worry and selfless support, her charismatic new tenant offers what Laura least expects: a second chance.

Darcy isn't surprised her mom doesn't understand her, though she never imagined her suddenly acting like a love-struck teen herself. With Troy starting to show signs of their father's bipolar disorder, and her best friend increasingly secretive, Darcy turns to her new boyfriend, Nick, for support. Yet Nick has a troubled side of his own, forcing Darcy toward life-altering choices.

Exploring the effects of grief on both mother and daughter, *Equilibrium* is a thoughtful, resolutely uplifting novel about finding the balance between holding on and letting go, between knowing when to mourn and when to hope, and between the love we seek and the love we choose to give.

"*Equilibrium is an emotional, complex, and deeply satisfying novel about the power of hope, love, and family. I couldn't put it down!*" —**Lisa Verge Higgins, author of *One Good Friend Deserves Another***

"*Tender, heartbreaking and beautifully realistic. Fans of Anita Shreve will be riveted by this intense and compassionate story.*" —**Hank Phillippi Ryan, Agatha, Anthony and Macavity-winning author**

ABOUT THE AUTHOR: **Lorrie Thomson** lives in New Hampshire with her husband and their children. When she's not reading, writing, or hunting for collectibles, her family lets her tag along for camping adventures, daylong paddles, and hikes up 4,000 footers.

September 2013 | Trade Paperback | Fiction | 336 pp | $15.00 | ISBN 9780758285775
Kensington Books | kensingtonbooks.com | lorrie-thomson.com

CONVERSATION STARTERS

1. How does Darcy see her mother at the beginning of the novel? Discuss the ways in which that perspective changes by the end. Talk about how Laura and Darcy switch roles over the course of the story.

2. Jack used to tell Laura that the most obvious reasons for a character's actions were usually wrong, excuses masquerading as explanation. How does this apply to Laura's relationship with Aidan? Laura says that Aidan is the polar opposite of her late husband. Do you think this makes him a good match for Laura? Why?

3. How does Troy deal with his grief over Jack's death? Laura believes she and her son are very much alike. Do you agree?

4. When Darcy first meets Nick, she thinks of herself as Daddy's girl. Even though she's embarrassed by how her father ended his life, she's always looked up to him. Has her relationship with her father changed by the end of the story? How?

5. Laura mentions her mother, a woman who kept to herself and might've died from never having reached out to others. Do you think Laura sees herself in her mother? Are there similarities? By the story's end, how has she learned to take her mother's life as a lesson in reverse?

6. How had Laura tamped down her emotions in response to Jack's? Is that coping mechanism now working in her favor or against her?

7. At the beginning of the story, Darcy's best friend Heather is struggling with a secret that she later reveals to Darcy. The reveal forces a temporary wedge between them. How do keeping secrets, and the resulting fallout, factor into other aspects of the story?

8. As an adult, how does Laura now view the way her relationship with Jack began? How does that factor into her romance with Aidan?

9. In what ways do Elle and Maggie support Laura? Why is Laura reluctant to tell them about her relationship with Aidan?

10. Laura stuck by Jack through his struggles with bipolar disorder. Do you have any personal experience with it? If so, how has that influenced the way you read *Equilibrium*? Do you think she could have—or should have—done anything different with Jack?

FLIGHT BEHAVIOR

Barbara Kingsolver

Dellarobia Turnbow is a restless farm wife who gave up her own plans when she accidentally became pregnant at seventeen. Now, after a decade of domestic disharmony on a failing farm, she seeks momentary escape through an obsessive flirtation with a younger man.

She hikes up a mountain road behind her house toward a secret tryst, but instead encounters a shocking sight: a silent, forested valley filled with what looks like a lake of fire. She can only understand it as a cautionary miracle, but it sparks a raft of other explanations from scientists, religious leaders, and the media. The bewildering emergency draws rural farmers into unexpected acquaintance with urbane journalists, opportunists, sightseers, and a striking biologist with his own stake in the outcome.

As the community lines up to judge the woman and her miracle, Dellarobia confronts her family, her church, her town, and a larger world, in a flight toward truth that could undo all she has ever believed.

"A majestic and brave new novel . . . both intimate and enormous."
—The New York Times Book Review

ABOUT THE AUTHOR: **Barbara Kingsolver**'s work has been translated into more than twenty languages and has earned a devoted readership at home and abroad. She was awarded the National Humanities Medal, our country's highest honor for service through the arts. She received the 2011 Dayton Literary Peace Prize for the body of her work, and in 2010 won Britain's Orange Prize for *The Lacuna*. Her novel *The Poisonwood Bible* was a finalist for the Pulitzer Prize. Before she made her living as a writer, Kingsolver earned degrees in biology and worked as a scientist. She now lives with her family on a farm in southern Appalachia.

June 2013 | Trade Paperback | Fiction | 464 pp | $16.99 | ISBN 9780062124272
Harper Perennial | harpercollins.com | kingsolver.com

CONVERSATION STARTERS

1. What is the significance of the novel's title? Talk about the imagery of flight. How is it represented throughout the story?

2. How do the chapter titles relate both to scientific concepts as well as the events that unfold within each chapter itself?

3. Describe Dellarobia. How is she of this mountain town in Tennessee and how is she different from it? How are she and her family connected to the land and to nature itself? How are they disconnected? How does this shape their viewpoints? How does she describe herself? Do you agree with her self-assessment?

4. Talk about the characters names—Dellarobia, Preston, Cordelia, Dovey, Ovid Byron, Cub, Bear, Hester. How does the author's choice of nomenclature suit her characters? When you first met these characters, including Pastor Bobby, what were your first impressions? Were your notions about them challenged as the story progressed?

5. How does Della react when she first sees the Monarchs? What greater meaning do the butterflies hold for her? How is she like the butterflies? How does finding them transform her life? Were the butterflies a miracle?

6. As news of her discovery spreads, what are the reactions of her in-laws and her neighbors? How do they view Della? What are their impressions of the scientists and tourists who descend upon their remote town?

7. What does Dellarobia think about her new friends, and especially Ovid Byron? What about the scientists—how do they view people like Della, her family, and her neighbors? Does either side see they other realistically?

8. Though she may not have a formal education beside her high school diploma, would you call Dellarobia wise? Where does her knowledge come from? Is she religious? Their Christian faith is very important to many of her neighbors. How does Barbara Kingsolver portray religion, faith, and God in the novel? What are your impressions of Pastor Bobby?

9. Why do so many Americans fear or dislike science? Why do so many others fear or dislike religion? What impact do these attitudes have on the nation now and what do they portend for our future?

GARDEN OF STONES

Sophie Littlefield

In the dark days of war, a mother makes the ultimate sacrifice . . .

Lucy Takeda is just fourteen years old, living in Los Angeles, when the bombs rain down on Pearl Harbor. Within weeks, she and her mother, Miyako, are ripped from their home, rounded up— along with thousands of other innocent Japanese-Americans—and taken to the Manzanar prison camp. Buffeted by blistering heat and choking dust, Lucy and Miyako must endure the harsh living conditions of the camp. Corruption and abuse creep into every corner of Manzanar, eventually ensnaring beautiful, vulnerable Miyako. Ruined and unwilling to surrender her daughter to the same fate, Miyako soon breaks. Her final act of desperation will stay with Lucy forever . . . and spur her to sins of her own. Bestselling author Sophie Littlefield weaves a powerful tale of stolen innocence and survival that echoes through generations, reverberating between mothers and daughters. It is a moving chronicle of injustice, triumph, and the unspeakable acts we commit in the name of love.

*"By looking at the effects of internment across generations, Littlefield makes her tale resonant and universal. . . . (a) gripping story unfolding over two different decades." —***Publishers Weekly**

*"A remarkable work of fiction. . . Reading this dramatic, affecting account is an illuminating and insightful journey." —***Bookreporter.com**

*"A moving drama of women in a Japanese American family over the course of three generations. . . . The shocking revelation is unforgettable." —***Booklist**

About the Author: **Sophie Littlefield** grew up in rural Missouri and attended college in Indiana. She worked in technology before having children, and was lucky enough to stay home with them while they were growing up. She writes novels for kids and adults and lives in Northern California.

March 2013 | Trade Paperback | Fiction | 320 pp | $14.95 | ISBN 9780778313526
Harlequin MIRA | harlequin.com | sophielittlefield.com

CONVERSATION STARTERS

1. After Pearl Harbor, many Americans worried that citizens of Japanese descent, especially those living on the West coast, might be acting as spies and traitors. Are such fears understandable? Can you think of similar events in recent history? How can we avoid reacting as we have in the past, with suspicion and intolerance?

2. The Takeda family was wealthier than many who were interned. Do you think that made the transition to camp life harder or easier? In what ways?

3. George Rickenbocker, Reg Forrest, and Benny Van Dorn created a sort of underground social network at Manzanar. How do you suppose they got away with it? How did internees figure into it? Do you think George and Benny were aware of Reg's involvement with Jessie, and if so, why did they tolerate it?

4. What finally drove Miyako to her desperate act in Manzanar? Do you feel she had other options, or was it the only way she could save Lucy?

5. In the deaths of George Rickenbocker and Reg Forrest, was justice served? Do you think Patty truly accepted the possibility that her mother killed Reg? Is she at peace with her mother's choices?

6. Patty grew up thinking her mother never experienced romantic love, but in fact, she did—twice: first with Jessie and then with Garvey. Why do you think Lucy continues to keep a few secrets, even after telling Patty nearly everything about her past?

7. Garvey is considerably older than Lucy. By contemporary standards, their relationship would be considered inappropriate. Do you think their relationship was genuine? Could they have survived in Lone Pine as a couple?

8. Taxidermy is more than an avocation for Garvey, and later, for Lucy. What is the symbolic significance of taxidermy in the novel? Why do you suppose each is drawn to it, and how does it bring them together?

9. Disfigurement is a recurring theme in the book. Besides Lucy, what other characters might be said to be wounded, either literally or figuratively?

10. There are several starkly different portrayals of motherhood in the novel. In what ways, if any, could each of these characters be considered good mothers?

GOOD KINGS BAD KINGS

Susan Nussbaum

**Pen/Bellwether Prize Winner
for Socially Engaged Fiction**

This powerful and inspiring debut invites us into a landscape populated with young people whose lives have been irreversibly changed by misfortune but whose voices resound with resilience, courage, and humor. Inside the halls of ILLC, an institution for juveniles with disabilities, we discover a place that is deeply different from and yet remarkably the same as the world outside. Nussbaum crafts a multifaceted portrait of a way of life hidden from most of us. In this isolated place on Chicago's South Side, friendships are forged, trust is built, and love affairs begin. It's in these alliances that the residents of this neglected community ultimately find the strength to bond together, resist their mistreatment, and finally fight back. And in the process, each is transformed.

*"Nussbaum wonderfully sweetens a stark subject with doses of idiosyncratic humor and hard-earned pathos . . . [she] upholds the individuality and integrity of her characters, never stooping to saccharine cliches or Hollywood manipulation . . . [a] moving story." —***The Wall Street Journal**

*"This is a world as foreign to most as another planet. That Nussbaum is able to make it as real and as painful and joyful and alive as she does is a spectacular accomplishment . . . a joy for readers." —***Chicago Tribune**

*"This is fiction at its best. . . . The story's sharp eye allows no one to take shelter, and it doesn't flinch. . . . A stunning accomplishment." —***Barbara Kingsolver**

*"Saucy, brutally funny, gritty, profane, poignant and real." —***The Kansas City Star**

ABOUT THE AUTHOR: **Susan Nussbaum**'s plays have been widely produced. Her play *Mishuganismo* is included in the anthology *Staring Back: The Disability Experience from the Inside Out.* In 2008 she was cited by the *Utne Reader* as one of "50 Visionaries Who Are Changing Your World" for her work with girls with disabilities. This is her first novel.

November 2013 | Trade Paperback | Fiction | 320 pp | $14.95 | ISBN 9781616203252
Algonquin Books | workman.com

CONVERSATION STARTERS

1. Discuss the title of the book. How does this title relate to various characters in the novel?

2. Discuss the relationship of Jimmie and Yessie. What does Jimmie derive from their relationship? What does Yessie get from Jimmie?

3. How do the characters with disabilities in this book compare with similar characters in other books you've read?

4. Why do you think the author used a first-person narrator approach to telling the story?

5. Is it unusual to hear characters with disabilities tell their own stories? Why or why not? How might this impact the way you view people with disabilities in real life?

6. How does Joanne's perspective on things change over the course of the novel, and why? Does she think differently about love? About her disability? About her ability to change things?

7. The book makes the argument that institutionalization is cruel and inhuman. Why does our society continue to rely so heavily on institutionalization as a resource for children with disabilities?

8. The book makes the argument that abuse and neglect are a natural outcome of the institutional structure. Do you think institutions such as the Illinois Learning and Life Skills Center are still reasonable living alternatives for people with disabilities? What are some other possible alternatives to institutionalization?

9. What role does paternalism play in the lives of people with disabilities? Can you give some examples?

10. The book talks a lot about jobs: job discrimination, jobs with low pay, overwork, relationships with coworkers, past jobs, and even possible future jobs. How important is your job in your life? Since more than 70 percent of people with disabilities experience chronic unemployment, how might this affect their adult lives?

11. If you could predict what some of the characters' lives would be like ten years from now, what might they be doing and where would they be? Yessenia? Jimmie? Louie? Pierre? Mia?

12. There is frequent debate concerning whether white writers can authentically represent characters of other races in their work. People with disabilities often complain that books written by writers without disabilities can't authentically represent characters with disabilities. Considering this book and others, what's your opinion on this issue?

THE GOOD LIFE

Susan Kietzman

Between workouts, charity events, and shopping, Ann Barons keeps her days as full as her walk-in closets. She shares an immaculate house with her CEO husband, Mike, and their two teenagers, Nate and Lauren. It's a luxurious life, far from her home-spun childhood on a farm in eastern Pennsylvania, which is why Ann is wary when her elderly parents ask to move in temporarily.

Ann prepares in the way she knows best—hiring decorators and employing a full-time nurse for her dementia-stricken father. But nothing can prepare her for the transformations ahead. Soon, her mother Eileen is popping in to prepare soups and roasts in Ann's underused kitchen, while the usually surly Nate forms an alliance with his ailing grandfather. Lauren blossoms under Eileen's guidance, and even workaholic Mike finds time to attend high-school football games. But it's Ann who must make the biggest leap, and confront the choices and values that have kept her floating on life's surface for so long.

Timely, poignant, and wise, *The Good Life* is a deeply satisfying and beautifully written story about the complex relationships between parents and children—and the gap that often lies between what we seek, and what will truly make us whole.

"The moving story of a family's rebirth through the simple but profound acts of daily kindness and sacrifice." —**Holly Chamberlin, author of *Last Summer***

ABOUT THE AUTHOR: **Susan Kietzman** is a Connecticut native. She has a bachelor's degree in English from Connecticut College and a master's degree in journalism from Boston University. She has worked in both magazine and newspaper publishing and currently writes grants for the Mystic Seaport Museum. *The Good Life* is her first novel. She lives with her family in Mystic, Connecticut.

March 2013 | Trade Paperback | Fiction | 352 pp | $15.00 | ISBN 9780758281326
Kensington Books | kensingtonbooks.com | susankietzman.com

CONVERSATION STARTERS

1. Ann appears to have had a fairly happy childhood, growing up on a farm in Pennsylvania. What do you think turns her away from it as an adult?

2. Ann is attracted to Mike in college because he is "great looking and powerful." Why is Mike attracted to Ann, especially since he might be able to choose from a large pool of young women? Ann and Mike come from very different backgrounds; what do they have in common?

3. Nate and Lauren are pretty typical teenagers, sometimes sarcastic and surly, sometimes withdrawn and insecure. With a workaholic and an avid shopper as role models, why aren't Nate and Lauren insufferable? Or are they?

4. When Sam and Eileen move in, why are Nate and Lauren drawn to them? What do Sam and Eileen provide that Mike and Ann do not?

5. Sam's Parkinson's disease and dementia unnerve Mike, Ann, Nate, and Lauren. How does each of them handle Sam's disabilities? How does Eileen treat her husband?

6. What kind of relationship did Ann anticipate having with her parents when they moved in? What happened to those expectations?

7. How does Ann's drinking fit in with her need for control? Why does Mike put up with her drinking? What happens when her drinking becomes an issue on the Florida trip with Jesse, Paula, and Sally?

8. Eileen seems to be a take-charge kind of person. Why does she often keep her thoughts to herself, instead of sharing them with her daughter? What, if anything, does Sam add to Ann's adult life?

9. When Eileen and Sam leave at the end of the book, who is most upset and why?

10. In the novel, who has the good life and who is still searching?

11. What does the good life mean to you?

A GUIDE FOR THE PERPLEXED

Dara Horn

The incomparable Dara Horn returns with a spell-binding novel of how technology changes memory and how memory shapes the soul.

Software prodigy Josie Ashkenazi has invented an application that records everything its users do. When an Egyptian library invites her to visit as a consultant, her jealous sister Judith persuades her to go. But in Egypt's post-revolutionary chaos, Josie is abducted—leaving Judith free to take over Josie's life at home, including her husband and daughter, while Josie's talent for preserving memories becomes a surprising test of her empathy and her only means of escape.

A century earlier, another traveler arrives in Egypt: Solomon Schechter, a Cambridge professor hunting for a medieval archive hidden in a Cairo synagogue. Both he and Josie are haunted by the work of the medieval philosopher Moses Maimonides, a doctor and rationalist who sought to reconcile faith and science, destiny and free will. But what Schechter finds, as he tracks down the remnants of a thousand-year-old community's once-vibrant life, will reveal the power and perils of what Josie's ingenious work brings into being: a world where nothing is ever forgotten.

An engrossing adventure that intertwines stories from Genesis, medieval philosophy, and the digital frontier, *A Guide for the Perplexed* is a novel of profound inner meaning and astonishing imagination.

"What do computerized data storage, sibling rivalry, the Book of Ruth, and Egyptian uncertainty after the Arab Spring have in common? They're all part of this latest work about two crucial aspects of being human: the ability to remember and to love. Horn has already proven herself by being named one of Granta's Best Young American Novelists and winning two National Jewish Book Awards. A sure bet." —**Library Journal**

About the Author: **Dara Horn**, the author of the novels *All Other Nights*, *The World to Come*, and *In the Image*, is one of *Granta*'s "Best Young American Novelists" and the winner of two National Jewish Book Awards.

September 2013 | Hardcover | Fiction | 352 pp | $25.95 | ISBN 9780393064896
W. W. Norton & Company | wwnorton.com | darahorn.com
Sign up for the Norton newsletter & giveaways: http://bit.ly/wwnorton-reading-group-guides

CONVERSATION STARTERS

1. Josie's Genizah software categorizes memories by themes like "entertainment" and "travel" and carefully curates what it records to bury the unpleasant and the ugly. Do our minds work this way? Would you subscribe to Genizah? How has other technology already changed how you experience things and remember them?

2. What is the significance of dreams in the novel? Does it make sense to catalog them in Genizah along with daytime memories, as Nasreen wants to do? Do you think they are "mental garbage" or "a window to a world beyond what a waking person could perceive"?

3. Josie designed her software to record patterns in human behavior, which she thinks can be used to predict future outcomes. Maimonides believed that, as the ancient rabbis expressed it, "Everything is foreseen, but freedom of choice is granted." Are their beliefs compatible? Do you believe that you are in control of the choices you make?

4. One of Cairo's unique features is its vast necropolis full of living squatters, but Nasreen says, "All cities are really cities of the dead." Do you agree with her? Do you live in a place where you can feel the generations that came before you?

5. In what ways does the novel's narrative parallel the biblical story of Joseph? Do you think this correspondence enhances the power of the novel? In general, are biblical stories relevant to the present or to understanding the challenges of modern life?

6. Did Judith deserve Josie's forgiveness in the end? Did Josie deserve Judith's? Did the final chapter about Tali change the way you felt about the outcome of the story?

7. Like historians piecing together the past, several characters wish to bring the dead back "to life" through bits of memory, writings, photographs, and recordings. Is this possible? How have you dealt with the death of someone you loved and the artifacts—such as letters and photographs—that were left behind?

8. How do the three stories—of Josie and Judith Ashkenazi, Solomon Schechter, and Mosheh ben Maimon—intersect and relate to one another? How does Maimonides's *Guide for the Perplexed* echo through all the layers of the novel?

HAPPIER AT HOME

Kiss More, Jump More, Abandon a Project, Read Samuel Johnson, and My Other Experiments in the Practice of Everyday Life

Gretchen Rubin

One Sunday afternoon, as she unloaded the dishwasher, Gretchen Rubin felt hit by a wave of homesickness. Homesick—why? She was standing right in her own kitchen. She felt homesick, she realized, with love for home itself. "Of all the elements of a happy life," she thought, "my home is the most important." In a flash, she decided to undertake a new happiness project, and this time, to focus on home.

And what did she want from her home? A place that calmed her, and energized her. A place that, by making her feel safe, would free her to take risks. Also, while Rubin wanted to be happier at home, she wanted to appreciate how much happiness was there already.

So, starting in September (the new January), Rubin dedicated a school year —September through May—to making her home a place of greater simplicity, comfort, and love.

"Gretchen Rubin's inventive approach to creating a happier home life is as inspiring as it is informative. Happier At Home *is a soulful and enlightening guide for happiness-seekers of all stripes."*—**Cheryl Strayed, bestselling author of** **Wild**

About the Author: **Gretchen Rubin** is the author of several books, including the blockbuster #**1** *New York Times* bestseller *The Happiness Project*. Rubin started her career in law and was clerking for Supreme Court Justice Sandra Day O'Connor when she realized that she really wanted to be a writer. Raised in Kansas City, she lives in New York City with her husband and two daughters.

January 2014 | Trade Paperback | Memoir | 320 pp | $15.00 | ISBN 9780307886798
Three Rivers Press | CrownPublishing.com | happiness-project.com
Facebook.com/GretchenRubin | Twitter.com/GretchenRubin

CONVERSATION STARTERS

1. What does the term "home" mean to you? Do you agree with Rubin that it's one of the most important elements to your happiness? Do you have more than one place that you call "home"?

2. Rubin observes that for most people, "outer order contributes to inner calm," and many of her resolutions are aimed at clutter-clearing. Are you affected by clutter—or not?

3. Rubin describes her struggle to conquer her fear of driving. Have you faced a similar challenge, when you've felt anxious about something that other people seem to take for granted (e.g., speaking in front of a group, flying, riding in a ski-lift)?

4. Do you have any "shrines" in your home? If you were going to make one, what would you include?

5. Rubin describes the three types of happiness leeches: grouches, jerks, and slackers. Do you have happiness leeches in your life? Have you found ways to insulate yourself from the negative emotions these leeches can spread?

6. If you decided to "suffer for fifteen minutes," what big task might you tackle?

7. *Happier at Home* is packed with quotations. Which quotation resonated most with you?

8. Rubin repeatedly emphasizes that she wants to find more happiness in her everyday life, and much of her happiness project is aimed at very small, ordinary aspects of her daily routine. Do you agree or disagree with this "little things" approach?

9. If a new room magically appeared in your house or apartment, how would you use it? Is there a way you could make your current place reflect that use now?

10. Did reading this book make you want to try any resolutions? Which ones?

11. Rubin's discussion of happiness is rooted in her own experience. She doesn't address the experience of people in different countries, different eras, or different circumstances. Did you find this approach narrow? Or was it helpful to see the theories of happiness tested against the experience of a particular person?

A HOLOGRAM FOR THE KING

Dave Eggers

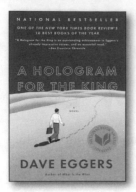

A National Book Award Finalist

One of the *The New York Times Book Review*'s 10 Best Books of the Year

One of the Best Books of the Year from *The Boston Globe* and *San Francisco Chronicle*

In a rising Saudi Arabian city, far from weary, recession-scarred America, a struggling businessman named Alan Clay pursues a last-ditch attempt to stave off foreclosure, pay his daughter's college tuition, and finally do something great. In *A Hologram for the King*, Dave Eggers takes us around the world to show how one man fights to hold himself and his splintering family together.

"*A Hologram for the King is an outstanding achievement in Eggers's already impressive career, and an essential read.*" —**San Francisco Chronicle**

"*[A] clear, supremely readable parable of America in the global economy that is haunting, beautifully shaped, and sad. . . . A story human enough to draw blood. . . . Groundbreaking.*" —**The New York Times Book Review**

"*Completely engrossing. . . . Perfect.*" —**Fortune**

"*Dave Eggers is a prince among men. . . . A strike against the current state of global economic injustice.*" —**Vanity Fair**

ABOUT THE AUTHOR: **Dave Eggers** is the bestselling author of *Zeitoun*, winner of the American Book Award and Dayton Literary Peace Prize. His novel *What Is the What* was a finalist for the National Book Critics Circle Award and won France's Prix Medici.

June 2013 | Trade Paperback | Fiction | 352 pp | $15.95 | ISBN 9780307947512
Vintage | randomhouse.com

CONVERSATION STARTERS

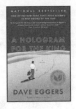

1. In the first few pages, we learn many things about Alan Clay. Do you feel distant from Alan, or do you feel empathy for him? Does your response to him change as the novel proceeds? Can you think of similar protagonists in other novels you have read?

2. What does Charlie's suicide mean to Alan, and why does he keep thinking about it?

3. What has caused the decline of Alan's career? Is there any way he might have averted the situation in which he now finds himself?

4. Is Alan's life exemplary of the crisis in American identity?

5. How is digital technology—which Alan is now trying to sell to King Abdullah—different from the creation and export of manufactured things? How do the young people Alan is working with on the hologram presentation differ from him in their assumptions about work and business?

6. Hanne gives Alan some contraband alcohol, which he enjoys alone in his hotel room. How do Alan's alcohol-fueled reflections affect the mood of the novel? Why is Alan surprised by what he sees at the embassy party Hanne takes him to?

7. How does he respond to the physical presence of his doctor, Zahra Hakem?

8. To what degree are Alan's difficulties in the present related to his marriage to his ex-wife, Ruby? How has his failed marriage affected his relationship with his daughter?

9. What does Alan learn about the realities of life in the Kingdom of Saudi Arabia through his conversations with Hasan, Yousef, and Yousef's friends?

10. How does Alan manage to nearly kill the shepherd boy, and what does he learn about himself in that moment?

11. What function does Alan's mental letter to his daughter serve in his own mind? What is he trying to communicate to her? Does their trip to see the launch of the space shuttle Atlantis show him to be a good father?

12. When the benign cyst is removed from Alan's neck, he feels confused. Does the fact that there is nothing physically wrong with him imply that he will now feel better psychologically?

13. Alan finally does make his presentation to King Abdullah. How does the ending work and what response does it create in you?

I'LL BE SEEING YOU

Suzanne Hayes and Loretta Nyhan

"I hope this letter gets to you quickly. We are always waiting, aren't we? Perhaps the greatest gift this war has given us is the anticipation..."

It's January 1943 when Rita Vincenzo receives her first letter from Glory Whitehall. Glory is an effervescent young mother, impulsive and free as a bird. Rita is a sensible professor's wife with a love of gardening and a generous, old soul. Glory comes from New England society; Rita lives in Iowa, trying to make ends meet. They have nothing in common except one powerful bond: the men they love are fighting in a war a world away from home. Brought together by an unlikely twist of fate, Glory and Rita begin a remarkable correspondence. The friendship forged by their letters allows them to survive the loneliness and uncertainty of waiting.

*"Engaging, charming and moving, a beautifully rendered exploration of WWII on the homefront and the type of friendship that helps us survive all manner of battles." —**Kirkus Review***

"A delight! I'll Be Seeing You *made me want to get out a pen and paper and write a friend a good old-fashioned letter."* —**Sarah Jio, author of** *The Violets of March*

"A compelling story of two women who endured, bolstered by duty, love and, most important, friendship. I read this sweet, compassionate novel with my heart in my throat." —**Kelly O'Connor McNees, author of** *The Lost Summer of Louisa May Alcott*

"Vivid and well-crafted, I'll Be Seeing You *poignantly illustrates the hopes and struggles of life on the home front. Readers will laugh, cry and be inspired by this timeless story of friendship and courage."* —**Pam Jenoff, bestselling author of** *The Kommandant's Girl*

ABOUT THE AUTHOR: **Suzanne Hayes** and **Loretta Nyhan** wrote *I'll Be Seeing You*, the story of two women connecting with each other via letters during WWII, during an intense flurry of emails over a six-month period.

June 2013 | Trade Paperback | Fiction | 336 pp | $15.95 | ISBN 9780778314950
Harlequin MIRA | harlequin.com

CONVERSATION STARTERS

1. Rita and Glory's friendship was born of intimacy, even though they don't know each other before they begin writing. The definition of intimacy is "shared fear." How does this explain the depth of their friendship? Have you ever had a close friend with whom you shared fear? If so, how is that friendship different from others you have?

2. Rita and Glory are very different people. They are from different parts of the country, they are not the same age and they come from different social classes. They also share similarities with each other: motherhood, community, a strong sense of women's rights. Did you identify with one or the other character because of their similarities, or because of their differences? Which one, and why?

3. Glory and Rita spend a lot of time in their letters talking about their victory gardens. The gardens become a metaphor in the novel. What are some of the things the gardens represent? Was anyone inspired to plant their very own victory garden?

4. The romance between Levi and Glory is complicated. They were friends, childhood sweethearts, and then they were both left behind when Robert went to war. Why do you think Glory let the romance go as far as it did? Can you sympathize with her actions? How do you feel about how the love triangle was ultimately resolved?

5. Social historians have often noted the importance of the women who went to work during wartime, seeing them as the root of the women's equal rights movement later in the twentieth century. How do the female characters in *I'll Be Seeing You* illustrate this? In what ways is it similar or different today?

6. To a certain extent, most of the characters are waiting for something (oftentimes, multiple things). Besides waiting for their men to come home, what else are Glory and Rita waiting for? How about some of the other characters? Do you feel the wait is worth it?

7. A few of the letters are marked Unsent. Why do you think the women decided not to send these particular letters? How would their stories change if they had? What do the unsent letters reveal about Glory and Rita's characters?

IS THIS TOMORROW

Caroline Leavitt

In the dark days of war, a mother makes the ultimate sacrifice . . .

In 1956, Ava Lark rents a house with her twelve-year-old son, Lewis, in a desirable Boston suburb. Ava is beautiful, divorced, Jewish, and a working mom. She finds her neighbors less than welcoming. Lewis yearns for his absent father, befriending the only other fatherless kids: Jimmy and Rose. One afternoon, Jimmy goes missing. The neighborhood—in the throes of Cold War paranoia—seizes the opportunity to further ostracize Ava and her son.

Years later, when Lewis and Rose reunite to untangle the final pieces of the tragic puzzle, they must decide: Should you tell the truth even if it hurts those you love, or should some secrets remain buried?

"Leavitt has a way of crafting the loveliest novels out of tragedy . . . It's her examination of loss, grief, and disappointment that will engross readers." —**Booklist**

"In her dynamite follow-up to Pictures of You, *Caroline Leavitt has given us that rare and irresistible combination of tenderly crafted, richly layered, and utterly believable characters—people I found myself caring about by page ten—and a crackling suspense story that just explodes off the page. Call it a literary thriller:* Is This Tomorrow *reveals a world you will want to linger in and secrets you'll stay up late to untangle."* —**Joyce Maynard**

"A beautiful, free-spirited divorcee is shunned by her neighbors; a boy from that neighborhood goes missing: this is the engine that drives Leavitt's latest story, a page-turner from first to last. I loved the way Leavitt's Mad Men–*like examination of shifting mid-century American values dovetails with her vivid tale of heartbreak and hope."* —**Wally Lamb**

ABOUT THE AUTHOR: **Caroline Leavitt** is the award-winning author of eight novels. Her essays and stories have been included in *New York* magazine, *Psychology Today*, *More*, *Parenting*, *Redbook*, and *Salon*. She is a columnist for the *Boston Globe*, a book reviewer for *People*, and a writing instructor at UCLA online.

May 2013 | Trade Paperback | Fiction | 384 pp | $14.95 | ISBN 9781616200541
Algonquin Books | workman.com | carolineleavitt.com

CONVERSATION STARTERS

1. Why do you think Leavitt takes a child-vanishing story and sets it in the 1950s? What does the era add to the story? Would the story have had a different outcome if it were set in a different time frame?

2. The title, *Is This Tomorrow*, was the actual name of a lurid 1950s-era pamphlet about the threat of Communism, but the title works on other levels in the novel. Why else do you think Leavitt gave the novel that title?

3. So much of *Is This Tomorrow* is about what it means to be a part of a community and how difficult it is to be an outsider. Who besides Ava and Lewis are outsiders? How does an outsider affect both Ava and Lewis at work and in their relationships?

4. Leavitt's novel probes the directions our lives can take. Lewis and Jimmy have an actual map to guide them in future trips. Lewis has no sense of direction, and at one point Ava tells him to watch for and read the signs and he won't get lost. What do you think are some of the important signs in Lewis's life, and how does Lewis follow or ignore them?

5. What are the different ways in which Lewis and Rose cope with Jimmy's disappearance, and how is each way integral to their personality? Who do you think has the most difficulty coping and why?

6. What makes Ava so suspect in the neighborhood, and would those things be suspect in any other era?

7. Although the novel is in the 1950s, what parallels do you see to contemporary life?

8. *Is This Tomorrow* is very much about fathers and sons and mothers and sons. How does Lewis's relationship with his father and with Ava change throughout the novel?

9. Why is being a nurse the perfect job for Lewis? And why does he begin to move away from it?

10. Why and how do all the characters feel guilt in one way or another for something they could have or should have done?

11. Who does Leavitt lead you to suspect is responsible for what happens to Jimmy? How many different people did you suspect and why?

JUST LIKE OTHER DAUGHTERS

Colleen Faulkner

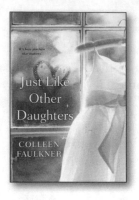

Alicia Richards loved her daughter from her very first breath. Days later, when tests confirmed what Alicia already knew—that Chloe had Down syndrome—she didn't falter. Her ex-husband wanted a child who would grow to be a scholar. For Alicia, it's enough that Chloe just is.

Now twenty-five, Chloe is sweet, funny, and content. Alicia brings her to adult daycare while she teaches at a local college. One day Chloe arrives home thrumming with excitement, and says the words Alicia never anticipated. She has met someone—a young man named Thomas. Within days, Chloe and Thomas, also mentally challenged, declare themselves in love.

Alicia strives to see past her misgivings to the new possibilities opening up for her daughter. Shouldn't Chloe have the same right to love as anyone else? But there is no way to prepare for the relationship unfolding, or for the moments of heartbreak and joy ahead.

With grace and warmth, Colleen Faulkner tells an unflinching yet heart-rending story of mothers and daughters, and of the risks we all take, both in loving and in letting go.

"This deeply moving story of maternal love and renewal will touch your heart. It's a celebration of the capacity of the human heart to heal itself and embrace change, beautifully written with rare insight." —**Susan Wiggs, #1 *New York Times* bestselling author**

"Be prepared to weep tears of sorrow as well as tears of joy. This is a novel you won't soon forget." —**Holly Chamberlin, author of *Last Summer***

About the Author: **Colleen Faulkner** lives in Delaware where her family settled more than three hundred years ago. She comes from a long line of storytellers and spends her days, when she's not writing, running the family farm, reading, and traveling the world. She's still married to her high school sweetheart and has four children and two grandchildren.

November 2013 | Trade Paperback | Fiction | 288 pp | $15.00 | ISBN 9780758266842
Kensington Books | kensingtonbooks.com

CONVERSATION STARTERS

1. When the book opens, do you feel that Alicia is giving Chloe the independence she needs/deserves? If not, give an example.

2. Would you have responded differently than Alicia when Chloe first came home saying she and Thomas were going to get married?

3. Do you think Randall loved his daughter? Why do you think he wasn't more involved in her life? Was Alicia responsible for his lack of involvement? Do you think Randall's relationship with Chloe would have been different had Chloe not had an intellectual disability?

4. Do you think Alicia should have allowed Chloe to get married? Should Margaret have allowed Thomas to get married? Would there have been a better option?

5. Do you think having Chloe and Thomas move into Alicia's house after they were married was a good idea? Would the marriage have survived had they moved into Margaret's house? A group home?

6. How could Alicia have prevented Chloe and Thomas' marriage from failing? Margaret?

7. What would you have done if Chloe had been your daughter and become pregnant? How do you think others would have reacted to your choice?

8. How do you think Alicia's story will end?

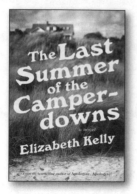

THE LAST SUMMER OF THE CAMPERDOWNS

Elizabeth Kelly

Set on Cape Cod during one tumultuous summer, Elizabeth Kelly's gothic family story will delight readers of *The Family Fang* and *The Giant's House*.

The Last Summer of the Camperdowns, from the best-selling author of *Apologize, Apologize!*, introduces Riddle James Camperdown, the twelve-year old daughter of the idealistic Camp and his manicured, razor-sharp wife, Greer. It's 1972, and Riddle's father is running for office from the family compound in Wellfleet, Massachusetts. Between Camp's desire to toughen her up and Greer's demand for glamour, Riddle has her hands full juggling her eccentric parents. When she accidentally witnesses a crime close to home, her confusion and fear keep her silent. As the summer unfolds, the consequences of her silence multiply. Another mysterious and powerful family, the Devlins, slowly emerges as the keepers of astonishing secrets that could shatter the Camperdowns. As an old love triangle, bitter war wounds, and the struggle for status spiral out of control, Riddle can only watch, hoping for the courage to reveal the truth. *The Last Summer of the Camperdowns* is poised to become the summer's uproarious and dramatic must-read.

"The plot unfolds like the Cape Cod season itself . . . beginning lazily, languidly, before heating up and morphing into a fast-paced thriller." —**Abbe Wright, O Magazine**

"Kelly's second novel is a witty, suspenseful tale of murder, marital conflict, and agonizing secrets...The exuberant story is transporting and delicious, a worthy summer read." —**Robin Micheli, People Magazine**

"Riveting. . . . Riddle perfectly narrates the events of one crazy, harrowing summer against the tumultuous backdrop of the 1970s. Written with cutting wit and intensity; it doesn't get any better than this." —**Library Journal**

ABOUT THE AUTHOR: **Elizabeth Kelly** is the best-selling author of the novel *Apologize, Apologize!* and is an award-winning journalist. She lives in Merrickville, Ontario, with her husband, five dogs, and three cats.

June 2013 | Hardcover | Fiction | 400 pp | $25.95 | ISBN 9780871403407
Liveright | wwnorton.com | lastsummerofthecamperdowns.com
Sign up for the Norton newsletter & giveaways: http://bit.ly/wwnorton-reading-group-guides

CONVERSATION STARTERS

1. The novel is set in Cape Cod during the summer of 1972. How does the physical setting and time period affect the story? How would the plot differ if the story was set in a different location at a different historical moment?

2. On numerous occasions throughout the novel, Riddle is compared to Greer. Are Riddle and Greer really as different as they appear? What qualities do they share?

3. As Michael reappears in the life of the Camperdowns, the relationship between Camp and Greer alters. Why does Michael change their dynamic, and what else could be at work between Camp and Greer?

4. How does Greer's experience as an actress influence her daily behavior? Although Greer is the only actress by profession, what other characters are guilty of performing their lives? What initiates their needs to play out specific roles?

5. Describe Riddle's relationship with Gula. How do you interpret Gula's fictitious stories that continue to unfold? Can you relate to Riddle's complicated emotions of perversion and seduction toward Gula?

6. Why do you think nineteen-year-old Harry has such an attachment to twelve-year-old Riddle? What is at the heart of their friendship?

7. What explains Gula's fascination with Riddle? Why do you think Gula gave Riddle the present at the end of the book?

8. In Charlie's book of condolences, Camp writes, "I will see you in the morning." What do you think this means?

9. Compare Michael and Camp; which man do you find more trustworthy? Whose account of the war do you believe? Who do you think Greer loved more?

10. How does the first chapter, set in the present, frame the rest of the novel that is set in the past? When the novel returns to the present in the epilogue, how have your feelings for Riddle changed from the beginning of the book?

11. The book is narrated from Riddle's point of view. How does her perspective influence the story? Do you trust her as a narrator? Why or why not?

12. Why do you think Riddle kept what she saw in the yellow barn a secret for so long? How was Gula able to manipulate Riddle to stay silent? What drove Riddle to finally reveal the truth?

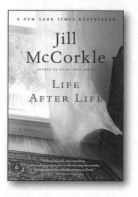

LIFE AFTER LIFE

Jill McCorkle

Award-winning author Jill McCorkle takes us on a splendid journey through time and memory in this, her tenth work of fiction. *Life After Life* is filled with a sense of wonder at our capacity for self-discovery at any age. And the residents, staff, and neighbors of the Pine Haven retirement center (from twelve-year-old Abby to eighty-five-year-old Sadie) share some of life's most profound discoveries and are some of the most true-to-life characters that you are ever likely to meet in fiction. Delivered with her trademark wit, Jill McCorkle's constantly surprising novel illuminates the possibilities of second chances, hope, and rediscovering life right up to the very end. She has conjured an entire community that reminds us that grace and magic can—and do—appear when we least expect it.

"Who knew death, regret, and lengthy ruminations about days past could add up to a novel this vibrant, hopeful, and compelling? . . . Gorgeously written . . . McCorkle's greatest gift is in illuminating the countless tiny moments that make up our time on Earth." —**O: The Oprah Magazine**

"Clever, bighearted, and wise." —**Vanity Fair**

"The elderly residents of Pine Haven live and yearn and challenge one another with an exuberance that jumps off the page." —**The New York Times** **"Home & Garden" section**

ABOUT THE AUTHOR: **Jill McCorkle** is the author of nine previous books—four story collections and five novels—five of which have been selected as *New York Times* Notable Books. The recipient of the New England Book Award, the John Dos Passos Prize for Excellence in Literature, and the North Carolina Prize for Literature, she teaches writing at North Carolina State University and lives in Hillsborough, North Carolina.

November 2013 | Trade Paperback | Fiction | 368 pp | $14.95 | ISBN 9781616203221
Algonquin Books | workman.com | jillmccorkle.com

CONVERSATION STARTERS

1. The structure of this novel is unusual, with its many voices and viewpoints. Why do you think the author chose to narrate the story this way?

2. If you were asked to name the novel's most central character, which would you choose? Why?

3. The last-moment-of-life monologues are interesting strokes of authorial imagination. How did you respond to them?

4. What does this novel imply about how people face death?

5. What are the societal consequences of remaining far removed from the process of dying?

6. How accurately do you think McCorkle portrays life in a continuing care retirement community?

7. How would you describe Sadie's influence on her fellow Pine Haven residents?

8. How do you respond to Toby's reasons for choosing Pine Haven? What about Rachel's reasons?

9. How did your perception of Stanley change throughout the novel? Did you approve or disapprove of the way he dealt with his son's involvement in his life? Why?

10. What about Marge? Does her characterization allow any room for the reader's empathy?

11. What is your perception of Abby's role in the novel?

12. Did you find any redeeming features in Kendra's characterization? What about in Ben's?

13. What do you imagine will become of Abby? What will become of Joanna? What about Sam Lowe?

14. Did the novel's ending surprise you? What ending might you have preferred?

LIFE AMONG GIANTS

Bill Roorbach

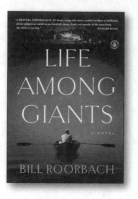

This funny, exuberant novel captures the reader with the grand sweep of seven-foot-tall David "Lizard" Hochmeyer's larger-than-life quest to unravel the mystery surrounding his parents' deaths. It's a journey laden with pro football stars, a master chef and his beautiful transvestite lover, a world-famous ballerina and her English rocker husband, and a sister who's as brilliant as she is unstable. A wildly entertaining, plot-twisting novel of murder, seduction, and revenge—rich in incident, expansive in character, and lavish in setting—*Life Among Giants* is an exhilarating adventure.

"*Consistently surprising and truly entertaining . . . Part thriller, part family drama,* Life Among Giants *is deliciously strange and deeply affecting.*" —*The Boston Globe*

"*A bighearted, big-boned story. . . .* Life Among Giants *reads like something written by a kinder, gentler John Irving. . . . Roorbach is a humane and entertaining storyteller with a smooth, graceful style.*" —**The Washington Post**

"*[Lizard's and his sister's] fascinating journey highlights the importance of steering your own fate, and it left me pondering where my own life will lead.*"—**Real Simple** (reader's review)

"*[An] eventful, elegiac novel of sports and murder, food and finance.*" —**Bloomberg News**

"*Hilarious and heartbreaking, wild and wise. . . .* Life Among Giants, *which is earning comparisons to* The World According to Garp, *is a vivid chronicle of a life lived large.*" —**Parade**

ABOUT THE AUTHOR: **Bill Roorbach** is the author of eight books of fiction and nonfiction. His work has been published in *Harper's, The Atlantic Monthly, Playboy, The New York Times Magazine, Granta,* and dozens of other magazines and journals.

August 2013 | Trade Paperback | Fiction | 352 pp | $14.95 | ISBN 9781616203245
Algonquin Books | workman.com | lifeamonggiantsthebook.com

CONVERSATION STARTERS

1. Who are the giants of the title? Is Lizard one of them, or is he merely an observer and chronicler? What is life among these giants like for Lizard? How have they steered his life? And how has he resisted them?

2. Why do you think Sylphide is so attracted to Lizard, and why, throughout their lives, does she keep him at arm's length? In what ways does he differ from the men she chooses to marry?

3. What is the draw of the High Side for each of the members of the Hochmeyer family? Is it something different for each one? Is there an equal repulsion for each? Who pays the highest price?

4. Is Lizard's father truly bad? Or is he an insecure person trying to build himself up? Is he being manipulated by stronger forces, or is he an operator, looking out for himself?

5. Lizard connects with a number of women in the book, yet he seems to pick loves who aren't truly available. What's that all about?

6. Emily is very important to Lizard, yet she doesn't offer herself to him very fully. Why does he hold her in such high regard? What role does she play in his development and in the development of the story?

7. How would you describe Lizard's relationship with Linsey? What about Sylphide's relationship with him, and Kate's? What is Linsey's role in the story?

8. Lizard takes warmly to Etienne and RuAngela. Why do you think this odd couple appeals to him?

9. From the first paragraph to the last climactic moments, food plays a big part in *Life Among Giants*. What is the role of food in the narrative?

10. Why does Sylphide choose death in the end? Hasn't she every reason to live?

11. What do you think Kate and Dabney's relationship was really like? Was it one based on love or was it based on something else?

12. *Life Among Giants* is not a traditional mystery, nor is it a traditional bildungsroman. How does it depart from the conventions of each genre? How does the story of this young man's growth interconnect with his quest to find the killers?

LOVE ANTHONY

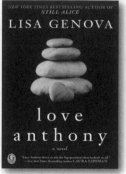

Lisa Genova

Olivia Donatelli's dream of a "normal" life shattered when her son, Anthony, was diagnosed with autism at age three. He didn't speak. He hated to be touched. He almost never made eye contact. And just as Olivia was starting to realize that happiness and autism could coexist, Anthony was gone.

Now she's alone on Nantucket, desperate to find meaning in her son's short life, when a chance encounter with another woman brings Anthony alive again in a most unexpected way.

In a warm, deeply human story reminiscent of *The Curious Incident of the Dog in the Night-time* and *Daniel Isn't Talking*, *New York Times* bestselling author Lisa Genova offers us two unforgettable women on the verge of change and the irrepressible young boy with autism whose unique wisdom helps them both find the courage to move on.

"Lisa Genova has essentially created her own genre, the 'Lisa Genova' novel, in which complicated topics become accessible to readers through beautifully-drawn characters and profound, human-scale stories. Love Anthony *dares to ask enormous questions, the big questions that bedevil all of us. Better yet, Genova has the wisdom to know which ones can be answered, and which cannot."* **—Laura Lippman, *The New York Times* bestselling author of *And When She Was Good***

About the Author: **Lisa Genova** graduated valedictorian from Bates College with a degree in biopsychology and holds a Ph.D. in neuroscience from Harvard University. She is a member of the Dementia Advocacy Support Network International and DementiaUSA and is an online columnist for the National Alzheimer's association. She lives with her husband and two children in Cape Cod. Her first two novels are the *New York Times* bestsellers *Still Alice* and *Left Neglected*.

April 2013 | Trade Paperback | Fiction | 336 pp | $16.00 | ISBN 9781439164693
Gallery Books | simonandschuster.com | lisagenova.com

CONVERSATION STARTERS

1. How much did you know about this condition before starting *Love Anthony*? Do you know anyone who has autism or an autistic person in their family?

2. What significance does the setting of Nantucket play in this story? Would the story have been different if it had taken place in New York City or Chicago?

3. Beth pulls a box out of her attic, filled with remnants from her old life, and is reminded of the woman she once was. If you were to go through a box from your attic, what items might you find?

4. On the subject of marriage and fidelity, Beth's friend Courtney muses: "You're always at the mercy of the people you're in a relationship with, right?" Do you agree? What do you think of the advice she offers Beth?

5. Do you think the author accurately captured the voice of a young autistic boy in the *Anthony* chapters? Did these sections enhance Beth's story for you? What about Olivia's journal entries?

6. Toward the end of the story, Olivia has an epiphany when she realizes that "There was more to Anthony's life than his death. And there was more to Anthony than his autism." What do you think finally enables Olivia to have this realization? Was it a singular event or a process?

7. When Jimmy and Beth share their homework assignments given to them by Dr. Campbell, were you surprised by Beth's initial reaction? Why is forgiving Jimmy the one thing Beth can't do?

8. Beth ultimately decides the lesson of her book is "Find someone to love and love without condition." Do you think this could also apply as an overall theme for *Love Anthony*? Can you find any others?

9. Which character did you relate to the most and why? Where do you see these characters in five years?

10. What do you think of Beth's epilogue? Do you think it provides a satisfying ending to her story? To the novel as a whole?

11. Another recurring theme of *Love Anthony* is faith—having faith, losing faith, and taking a leap of faith. Can you remember a time in your own life when you took a leap of faith?

LOVE WATER MEMORY

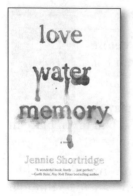

Jennie Shortridge

When missing Seattle woman Lucie Walker is found standing in the frigid San Francisco Bay with no recollection of her past, she must wake from the fog of amnesia to finally confront her darkest secrets. In this emotional drama, thirty-nine-year-old Lucie slowly uncovers what made her run away from a successful career and loving fiancé Grady, who struggles with his own emotional shortcomings and hides the details of his last encounter with Lucie. As Lucie struggles to reclaim her identity, she must first discover who she used to be, including finally unearthing the details of her tragic childhood.

*"This is a moving story told by a wonderful writer. It explores truth and love and reminds us that the people around us have helped form who we are, but in the end, the person we are capable of becoming is up to us." —**Real Simple***

"A wonderful book; lovely . . . just perfect." —**Garth Stein**, *The New York Times* bestselling author of *The Art of Racing in the Rain*

"Part tense mystery and part brilliant psychological drama, Shortridge's eloquent novel is a breathtaking story of how well we really know the people we love—and ourselves." —**Caroline Leavitt**, *The New York Times* bestselling author of *Pictures of You*

"Intriguing, resonant, and deeply satisfying, Love Water Memory *takes us into the mystery of one woman's past and her attempts to reclaim both herself and the love she left behind."* —**Erica Bauermeister, author of** *The School of Essential Ingredients*

ABOUT THE AUTHOR: **Jennie Shortridge** has published five novels: *Love Water Memory, When She Flew, Love and Biology at the Center of the Universe, Eating Heaven,* and *Riding with the Queen.* She is a founding member of Seattle7Writers.org, a collective of Northwest authors devoted both to raising funds for community literacy projects and to raising awareness of Northwest literature.

January 2014 | Trade Paperback | Fiction | 320 pp | $16.00 | ISBN 9781451684841
Gallery Books | simonandschuster.com | jennieshortridge.com

CONVERSATION STARTERS

1. Lucie suffers from dissociative fugue. According to the Cleveland Clinic, "The word fugue comes from the Latin word for 'flight.' People with dissociative fugue temporarily lose their sense of personal identity and impulsively wander or travel away from their homes or places of work. They often become confused about who they are and might even create new identities . . . Dissociative fugue has been linked to severe stress, which might be the result of traumatic events—such as war, abuse, accidents, disasters or extreme violence—that the person has experienced or witnessed." Discuss how the condition applies to Lucie.

2. Compare the pre-amnesiac Lucie with the "new" Lucie. How does she change, and what does this signify?

3. How does Grady's early family life affect his relationship with Lucie, and his own life choices? What role does his large, loquacious family play in the present-day story?

4. Lucie goes to great lengths to learn to cook after she comes home. What is the significance of food and the cooking scenes in the story?

5. Discuss the role of psychotherapy in the book, and each character's take on it. Why doesn't Lucie get help earlier? Can family members force their loved ones to seek counseling?

6. How did the death of a parent at a young age impact both Lucie and Grady? What are the similarities and differences in their experiences with love and loss, and how does early loss affect each one?

7. Compare the effect of music for Lucie, and water for Grady. What do they each find in those things, and why?

8. Helen longs to reconnect with her niece, yet is overwhelmed at having to tell Lucie the truth about the past. What contributes to her internal conflict?

9. In what ways is Grady holding on to his prior notions of the "old" Lucie? How does this affect his developing feelings for the "new" Lucie?

10. Discuss the similarities between Grady and Helen's deceased husband, Edward Ten Hands, and what drew Lucie to each of them.

11. How do you think Lucie will resolve her "new" and "old" selves?

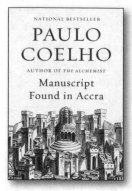

MANUSCRIPT FOUND IN ACCRA

Paulo Coelho

The latest novel from the #1 internationally bestselling author of *The Alchemist*, a parable about who we are, what we fear, and what we hope for in the future.

July 14, 1099. Jerusalem awaits the invasion of the crusaders who have surrounded the city's gates. There, inside the ancient city's walls, men and women of every age and every faith have gathered to hear the wise words of a mysterious man known only as the Copt. He has summoned the townspeople to address their fears, and allows them to ask a series of questions. They ask about defeat, struggle, and the nature of their enemies; they contemplate the will to change and the virtues of loyalty and solitude; and they ultimately turn to questions of beauty, love, wisdom, sex, elegance, and what the future holds.

"*His books have had a life-enhancing impact on millions of people.*" —*The Times*

"*His writing is like a path of energy that inadvertently leads readers to themselves, toward their mysterious and faraway souls.*" —**Le Figaro**

"*Coelho's writing is beautifully poetic but his message is what counts. . . . He gives me hope and puts a smile on my face.*" —**Daily Express**

"*An exceptional writer.*" —**USA Today**

ABOUT THE AUTHOR: One of the most influential writers of our time, **Paulo Coelho** is the author of many international best sellers, including *The Alchemist, Aleph, Eleven Minutes* and *The Pilgrimage*. Translated into 74 languages, his books have sold more than 140 million copies in more than 170 countries. He is a member of the Brazilian Academy of Letters, and in 2007, he was named a United Nations Messenger of Peace.

January 2014 | Trade Paperback | Fiction | 144 pp | $14.00 | ISBN 9780345805058
Vintage | randomhouse.com | paulocoelho.com

CONVERSATION STARTERS

1. "In the cycle of nature there is no such thing as victory or defeat; there is only movement." What do the cycles of the natural world teach us about the balance of difficult and rewarding moments in our lives?

2. "Solitude is not the absence of company, but the moment when our soul is free to speak to us and help us decide what to do with our life". Do the demands of everyday life (work, family, and other responsibilities) prevent people from examining insecurities or do these obligations, real and perceived, serve as an excuse for avoiding self-knowledge?

3. "We are afraid of change because we think that, after so much effort and sacrifice, we know our present world". How does the appeal—and comfort—of the familiar affect the choices we make? How can we reconcile our belief in the value of perseverance with the imperative to embrace change?

4. Why is the desire to give our lives meaning so strong? What role does the fear of death—the ultimate confrontation with the "Unwanted Visitor"—play?

5. What insights does the Copt offer into the nature of love between individuals? Does his assertion that "love is an act of faith, not an exchange" reflect your own experience? Does thinking of love this way make it easier to face disappointment or rejection?

6. "I will look at everything and everyone as if for the first time". Have you ever put aside habitual thoughts and emotions and viewed familiar surroundings through fresh eyes? What did you discover?

7. The Copt tells his listeners, "See sex as a gift, a ritual of transformation… Fearlessly open the secret box of your fantasies". How does this point of view compare with teachings about sex in traditional religions and spiritual practices? How does it both augment and extend the Copt's central message?

8. In what ways does the section on miracles evoke the tone and style of prayer? What does it illustrate about the connection between beliefs and behavior? About accepting the mysteries as well as the realities of life?

MARGOT

Jillian Cantor

In the spring of 1959, *The Diary of Anne Frank* has just come to the silver screen to great acclaim, and a young woman named Margie Franklin is working in Philadelphia as a secretary at a Jewish law firm. On the surface she lives a quiet life, but Margie has a secret: a life she once lived, a past and a religion she has denied, and a family and a country she left behind.

Margie Franklin is really Margot Frank, older sister of Anne, who did not die in Bergen-Belsen as reported, but who instead escaped the Nazis for America. But now, as her sister becomes a global icon, Margie's carefully constructed American life begins to fall apart. A new relationship threatens to overtake the young love that sustained her during the war, and her past and present begin to collide. Margie is forced to come to terms with Margot, with the people she loved, and with a life swept up into the course of history.

"Compassionate . . . A tour of the emotional nether land so often occupied by those who have survived the unimaginable and an example of extreme sibling competition—and love." —**Jenna Blum,** *The New York Times* **bestselling author of** *Those Who Save Us*

"Margot takes on big questions in an intimate story, and carefully considers whether it is possible to survive—and thrive—after unspeakable horror. A moving, affecting novel." —**Diana Abu-Jaber, author of** *Crescent* **and** *Birds of Paradise*

ABOUT THE AUTHOR: **Jillian Cantor** has a B.A. in English from Penn State University and an M.F.A. from the University of Arizona, where she was also a recipient of the national Jacob K. Javits Fellowship. The author of several books for teens and adults, she grew up in a suburb of Philadelphia. She currently lives in Arizona with her husband and two sons.

September 2013 | Trade Paperback | Fiction | 352 pp | $16.00 | ISBN 9781594486432
Riverhead Books | us.penguingroup.com | jilliancantor.com

CONVERSATION STARTERS

1. When Margot first meets Bryda, she introduces herself as Margie. What drives her to hide her full name and true identity? If she had confided in Bryda, how do you think the story would have changed?

2. Margie's uncertainty about the past illustrates how one's memory can change over time. How is Anne's diary and Margie's relationship to it affected by this truth?

3. Margie feels caged in by the past and does not embrace the new freedoms of being a woman in 1960s America. In contrast, Shelby relishes her growing freedom. How do these two opposing ideas of womanhood influence Margie's path over the course of the novel?

4. Margie's distinction between religion and ritual plays a big role in the novel. It is difficult for her to incorporate her religion into her American life. How does Margie's acceptance of her faith relate to her acceptance of her past and present?

5. Do you believe Margie's fantasy of a life with Pete in Levittown could ever happen? What do you think that life would be like for them? Would Margie ever embrace her old persona of "Margot," or would she remain Margie Franklin?

6. What centers Joshua's morality? We see him both defend criminals and go out of his way to take on cases his father denies because he feels a moral obligation. What drives that sense of obligation? How do we see his religion affecting his life and choices?

7. In many ways this is a novel about sisters. How do the feelings Margie has—both in the past and in the present—about Anne reflect the complicated nature of sister relationships? How does having and losing her sister impact her, in 1959 and beyond?

8. Does this fictionalized account affect your view of the Frank family and the real-life events surrounding the Holocaust?

9. Why do you think Margie is reluctant to reconnect with her father? What reasons does she have for avoiding contact? If she had contacted her father immediately upon learning he was alive, how do you think the story would have changed?

10. Margot Frank's diary was never recovered. If it had been, do you think it would have changed our understanding of the Holocaust and life inside the Annex for the Franks?

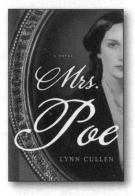

MRS. POE

Lynn Cullen

A vivid and compelling novel about a woman who becomes entangled in an affair with Edgar Allan Poe—at the same time she becomes the unwilling confidante of his much-younger wife.

It is 1845, and Frances Osgood is desperately trying to make a living as a writer in New York; not an easy task for a woman—especially one with two children and a philandering portrait painter as her husband.

She meets the handsome and mysterious Edgar Allan Poe at a literary party, and the two have an immediate connection. Poe wants Frances to meet with his wife since she claims to be an admirer of her poems, and Frances is curious to see the woman whom Edgar married.

As Frances spends more and more time with the intriguing couple, her intense attraction for Edgar brings her into dangerous territory. And Mrs. Poe, who acts like an innocent child, is actually more manipulative and threatening than she appears. As Frances and Edgar's passionate affair escalates, Frances must decide whether she can walk away before it's too late.

Set amidst the fascinating world of New York's literati, this smart and sexy novel offers a unique view into the life of one of history's most unforgettable literary figures.

"Mrs. Poe *has my heart racing. . . Don't miss it!*"—**Sara Gruen, *The New York Times* bestselling author of *Water for Elephants* and *Ape House***

"Mrs. Poe *is a compelling tale of ill-fated love, passion, and the writing life in antebellum New York, rich with period detail and suspense.*" —**Jennifer Chiaverini, *The New York Times* bestselling author of *Mrs. Lincoln's Dressmaker***

About the Author: **Lynn Cullen** grew up in Fort Wayne, Indiana, and is the author of *Reign of Madness*, a 2011 Best of the South selection by *The Atlanta Journal-Constitution* and *The Creation of Eve*, named among the best fiction books of 2010 by *The Atlanta Journal-Constitution*.

September 2013 | Hardcover | Fiction | 336 pp | $26.00 | ISBN 9781476702919
Gallery Books | simonandschuster.com | lynncullen.com

CONVERSATION STARTERS

1. Although Frances narrates the story, it is named for Mrs. Poe. Why do you think that Cullen has chosen to call the novel "*Mrs. Poe*"? Did the title affect your reading of the story? How?

2. After Frances meets Virginia Poe for the first time, Eliza asks her, "What does she seem like? Sweet? Sharp?," and Frances replies "Both, oddly enough." What does she mean? Do you agree with Frances's assessment of Virginia? Why or why not?

3. Miss Fuller tells Frances, "Beneath that pretty society-girl surface, you strike me as the striving sort." Do you agree? What reasons does Frances have to be "the striving sort"? What are your initial impressions of Frances? Did your feelings about Frances change throughout the novel? In what ways?

4. At one of the "*conversaziones*", Poe says, "Desire inspires us to be our very best." Do you agree? In what ways, if any, do Poe and Frances improve because of their relationship?

5. Were you surprised by Samuel's return? Although he is "maddeningly agreeable" with regard to Frances's relationship with Poe, he is critical of her work. After reading one of her poems, he tells her, "There was a time when you would have made fun of a poem like this." Why does Samuel's statement bother Frances so much? What do you think of the poem that he critiques?

6. Frances thinks that Virginia Poe is out to do her harm. What evidence supports her suspicions? Were you surprised when you found out the truth?

7. In several of his conversations with Frances, Poe makes references to stories that he has written, including "William Wilson" and "The Oval Portrait." How does Poe use these stories to communicate with Frances?

8. Poe reads "Al Aaraaf," the poem he wrote when he was fourteen, at the Boston Lyceum, claiming that he wanted "to see if they could tell the difference between a child's verse and a masterpiece." What do you think the real motivation behind his decision is? Do you agree with Mrs. Ellet that he called "down the wrath of the Boston circle" because it terrified him to do so? Why?

THE OCCUPATION OF ELIZA GOODE

Shelley Fraser Mickle

Eliza Goode is born into a New Orleans' parlor house in the mid-1800s. Sold as a courtesan on her seventeenth birthday, she flees her arranged future at the outbreak of the Civil War. She is passed up through Mississippi's plantations from one slave quarters to another until she emerges at the Confederates' Camp Corinth and is swept along to the battle of Manassas.

Along the way, she meets Bennett McFerrin and his wife, Rissa, who follows her husband to war. Using guile and her extraordinary beauty, Eliza transforms herself from camp follower and prostitute to laundress, nurse, and caregiver to Rissa when Bennett is taken prisoner by Ulysses S. Grant at the Battle of Fort Donelson in Clarksville, Tennessee. Her final transformation frees her from her past.

Eliza's story is more than a tale of war, transcendence, and hardship. It is a story told in modern times by Susan Masters, a novelist in Boston, whose cousin, Hadley, finds Eliza's letters in an attic and implores Susan to write Eliza's story to answer questions she seeks for her own life. Hadley has a shameful secret of her own—a past, about which she cannot even bring herself to speak.

Set in the second summer of the Iraq war and three years after 9/11, this is not your usual Civil War novel. This story says much about how we became who we are, and who we might have become, had the Civil War not saved us as a nation.

ABOUT THE AUTHOR: **Shelley Fraser Mickle** is an award-winning novelist and NPR commentator whose family history led her to the lifelong belief that one day she would write a Civil War novel. Shelley's debut novel was a *New York Times* Notable Book; her second became a CBS/Hallmark Channel movie; and her third became a suicide prevention tool in high schools, winning the 2006 Florida Governor's Award for suicide prevention in an educational setting. She is a nominee to the 2014 Florida Women's Hall of Fame.

November 2013 | Trade Paperback | Fiction | 300 pp | $17.95 | ISBN 9781938467691
Koehler Books | koehlerbooks.com | shelleymickle.com

CONVERSATION STARTERS

1. As the author researched the history for this novel, she passed on extraordinary information, such as that several in Lincoln's cabinet wanted to let the South go and expand into Canada, creating a separate nation with that land acquisition; also that germ warfare was attempted by trying to release a yellow fever epidemic in Washington, D.C. Did these facts astonish you too? Were there other facts that you learned, expanding your knowledge of the Civil War and your realization of how it changed America?

2. Hadley has a hard, sad life. When you learn what is driving her, is there information about her daily challenges that is new to you?

3. When Rissa dies and Eliza takes over Rissa's identity in the letters she writes to Bennett, do you view her act as immoral or generous? What are all the ways in which her act can be viewed? How much of loving someone is the desire to protect them?

4. There are many mothers in this story. How are they each different and what do they share: Eliza's mother, Hadley's mother, and then Hadley as a mother herself, as well as Eliza?

5. Susan realizes that Eliza was a marvelous storyteller, just as she attempts to be. Hadley places her faith in the power of story to inform her life. Is the power of story diminishing in our present culture? Are there stories that influence your life?

6. What in reading this book will you remember as part of your identity as an American?

"Shelley Fraser Mickle does it again. She writes a work of fiction that feels truer than non-fiction—a pager-turner that after the last page is turned, stays with you. Her stories are really about all of us and how our individual and collective history has changed us. And she does it with humor, compassion and lovely prose. As a member of a book club for 20 years, this will be my first recommendation. As a film producer, I say to all who are in love with story, you must read this book."
—**Dale Eldridge Kaye, CEO, Innovation Tri-Valley Leadership Group, Partner–Blind Pig Productions**

THE ORCHARDIST

Amanda Coplin

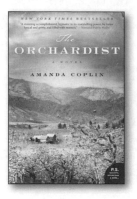

At the turn of the twentieth century, in a rural stretch of the Pacific Northwest, a reclusive orchardist, William Talmadge, tends to apples and apricots as if they were loved ones. A gentle man, he's found solace in the sweetness of the fruit he grows and the quiet, beating heart of the land he cultivates. One day, two teenage girls appear and steal his fruit at the market; they later return to the outskirts of his orchard to see the man who gave them no chase.

Feral, scared, and very pregnant, the girls take up on Talmadge's land and indulge in his deep reservoir of compassion. Just as the girls begin to trust him, men arrive in the orchard with guns, and the shattering tragedy that follows will set Talmadge on an irrevocable course not only to save and protect them but also to reconcile the ghosts of his own troubled past.

Transcribing America as it once was before railways and roads connected its corners, Amanda Coplin weaves a tapestry of solitary souls who come together in the wake of unspeakable cruelty and misfortune. She writes with breathtaking precision and empathy, and in *The Orchardist* she crafts an astonishing debut novel about a man who disrupts the lonely harmony of an ordered life when he opens his heart and lets the world in.

"Coplin is a masterful writer, the teller of an epic, unvarnished tale that sits comfortably with other novels in the tradition of great American story-telling." —**Wally Lamb, The New York Times bestselling author of *The Hour I First Believed***

ABOUT THE AUTHOR: **Amanda Coplin** was born in Wenatchee, Washington. She received her BA from the University of Oregon and MFA from the University of Minnesota. A recipient of residencies from the Fine Arts Work Center in Provincetown, Massachusetts, and the Omi International Arts Center at Ledig House in Ghent, New York, she lives in Portland, Oregon.

March 2013 | Trade Paperback | Fiction | 488 pp | $15.99 | ISBN 9780062188519
Harper Perennial | harpercollins.com

CONVERSATION STARTERS

1. How would you describe William Talmadge, the title character of *The Orchardist*? What adjective best describes his character? What are the factors that have shaped the man he is?

2. Though he is mostly alone, Talmadge has two good friends, the herbalist Caroline Middey and the Indian horse catcher Clee. What draws these three people together?

3. When Talmadge first meets the young sisters, Della and Jane, they are stealing his fruit. Why isn't he angry with them? Why does he want to help them? What does he see in them that others might not?

4. Talk about the sisters and the bond they share. Could most people survive the pain and shame of what they were forced to endure? What propels Jane's definitive act? What stops Della from following her? How do these choices reverberate in the years and events that follow?

5. Explore Della's character. Is she a good person? What drives her restlessness? Why is she driven by revenge? Why can't she find solace with Talmadge and Angelene in the orchard?

6. If he could articulate it, how would Talmadge define his relationship to Della? Do you think he thought of himself as Angelene's father? What about Angelene? Though he adored Angelene, "the emotion—the severity of it—also made him afraid." What was the root of Talmadge's fear? Why can love be simultaneously wondrous and terrifying?

7. Is there anything Talmadge could have—should have—done to keep Della with him and Angelene in the orchard? What hold did Della have on him? Did his concern for Della and his longing for her overshadow his relationship with Angelene?

8. Discuss Angelene and Della. How do they view one another? What kind of person does Angelene grow up to be? How might her life have been different if Della had been present?

9. Could you live as Talmadge did? Do you think he was lonely? Did he enjoy his solitude? What about Caroline, Clee, Della, Angelene? Were they lonely? How is being alone different from being lonely?

10. Late in the novel, Talmadge watches Angelene working in the cabin. "She was the dream of the place that bore her and she did not even know it." Explain what he means.

THE OTHER TYPIST

Suzanne Rindell

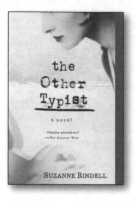

Rose Baker seals men's fates. With a few strokes of the keys that sit before her, she can send a person away for life in prison. A typist in a New York City Police Department precinct, Rose is like a high priestess. Confessions are her job. It is 1923, and while she may hear every detail about shootings, knifings, and murders, as soon as she leaves the interrogation room she is once again the weaker sex, best suited for filing and making coffee.

This is a new era for women, and New York is a confusing place for Rose. Gone are the Victorian standards of what is acceptable. All around her women bob their hair, they smoke, they go to speakeasies. Yet prudish Rose is stuck in the fading light of yesteryear, searching for the nurturing companionship that eluded her childhood. When glamorous Odalie, a new girl, joins the typing pool, despite her best intentions Rose falls under Odalie's spell. As the two women navigate between the sparkling underworld of speakeasies by night and their work at the station by day, Rose is drawn fully into Odalie's high-stakes world. And soon her fascination with Odalie turns into an obsession from which she may never recover.

*"Take a dollop of Alfred Hitchcock, a dollop of Patricia Highsmith, throw in some Great Gatsby flourishes, and the result is Rindell's debut, a pitch-black comedy about a police stenographer accused of murder in 1920s Manhattan. . . . A deliciously addictive, cinematically influenced page-turner, both comic and provocative."—**Kirkus Reviews**

ABOUT THE AUTHOR: **Suzanne Rindell is** a doctoral student in American modernist literature at Rice University. *The Other Typist* is her first novel. She lives in New York City and is currently working on a second novel.

April 2014 | Trade Paperback | Fiction | 368 pp | $16.00 | ISBN 9780425268421
Berkley Trade Paperback | us.penguingroup.com | suzannerindell.com

CONVERSATION STARTERS

1. Do you think Rose is a reliable or unreliable narrator? Why? If you did question her veracity, at what point in the novel did you begin to do so?

2. Why is Rose so captivated by Odalie, someone she wholly disapproves of initially?

3. Through Odalie, Rose gains entry into a world she's never seen before, one filled with opulence and rich, glamorous people. Clearly Rose is an outsider who doesn't belong. Yet she seems to take to it all rather quickly. Why do you think this is so? Why, despite all the new people she comes into contact with, is Odalie the only one she seems to be charmed by?

4. Some readers may think that Rose is a lesbian. Do you? Why or why not? Might her Victorian sensibility, when viewed by a contemporary reader, be misinterpreted and sexualized even if it might be innocent and pure?

5. Rose is such a stickler for the rules, yet as the novel progresses, she starts breaking them frequently. In retrospect, do you think she ever follows the rules? Or does she follow only the ones she agrees with?

6. Rose states in the beginning of the book: "I am there to transcribe what will eventually come to be known as the truth." The novel plays with the notion that the written word is superior to the spoken—Rose's transcripts and her diary that the reader is reading, versus the narration she provides throughout the book. Do you think the written word carries more weight than oral history? Why or why not?

7. What do you make of Rose's appearance? Throughout the novel she takes pains to point out that she is plain-looking. Yet the Lieutenant Detective obviously finds her attractive, and at the end of the book, she is a doppelgänger for Odalie, who is portrayed as a knockout. What do you think Rose really looks like? Should her appearance even matter?

8. When Rose is in the hospital at the end of the book, the doctors call her "Ginevra." That is the name Teddy used for Odalie. Who do you think is the real Ginevra? Are Odalie and Rose the same person?

9. What do you believe really happened at the end of the book? Did Rose kill Teddy? Or did Odalie?

THE PIECES WE KEEP

Kristina McMorris

In this richly emotional novel, Kristina McMorris evokes the depth of a mother's bond with her child, and the power of personal histories to echo through generations.

Two years have done little to ease veterinarian Audra Hughes's grief over her husband's untimely death. Eager for a fresh start, Audra plans to leave Portland for a new job in Philadelphia. Her seven-year-old son, Jack, seems apprehensive about flying—but it's just the beginning of an anxiety that grows to consume him. As Jack's fears continue to surface in recurring and violent nightmares, Audra hardly recognizes the introverted boy he has become. Desperate, she traces snippets of information unearthed in Jack's dreams, leading her to Sean Malloy, a struggling US Army veteran wounded in Afghanistan. Together they unravel a mystery dating back to World War II, and uncover old family secrets that still have the strength to wound—and perhaps, at last, to heal.

Intricate and beautifully written, *The Pieces We Keep* illuminates those moments when life asks us to reach beyond what we know and embrace what was once unthinkable. Deftly weaving together past and present, herein lies a story that is at once poignant and thought-provoking, and as unpredictable as the human heart.

"Gripped me from the first page and didn't let go." —**Alyson Richman, bestselling author of *The Lost Wife***

"The past collides with the present in this sensitive and multilayered story where the discovery of long-held family secrets leads to healing. The contemporary twist will be a treat for fans of World War II historical fiction." —**Beth Hoffman, *The New York Times* bestselling author of *Looking for Me* and *Saving CeeCee Honeycutt***

ABOUT THE AUTHOR: **Kristina McMorris** is an award-winning author and graduate of Pepperdine University. She currently resides in the Portland, Oregon where she is a member of several literary organizations including Willamette Writers, RWA®, and Rose City Romance Writers.

December 2013 | Trade Paperback | Fiction | 464 pp | $15.00 | ISBN 9780758281166
Kensington Books | kensingtonbooks.com | kristinamcmorris.com

CONVERSATION STARTERS

1. While reading *The Pieces We Keep*, did your interpretation of the title change over the course of the story?

2. What does "faith" mean to you? How did you come to arrive at that conclusion? Has a personal tragedy ever caused you to reexamine and/or alter your core beliefs?

3. Memories—cherished and burdensome, lost and recovered—are major elements of the book. Which memories in your life have played a distinct role in shaping your personality? If given a choice, would you erase any from your mind? How different might you be without them?

4. Connections between the past and present were interpreted by characters in different ways throughout the story. Early on, what did you perceive as the source of Jack's issues? Did that change by the book's end?

5. Do you believe in the possibility of past lives? In your opinion, does such a theory complement or contradict contemporary religious and/or Christian principles? Did the story reaffirm your existing beliefs or expand your thoughts about what might or might not be possible?

6. Every major character in the book wrestles with grief in some form. Discuss the range of ways in which each person deals with this emotion. Have you or your loved ones ever reacted to loss in a similar manner?

7. At several points in the novel, Audra questions her skeptical and spiritual beliefs. What is your personal view of coincidence versus fate or predestination?

8. How do secrets, whether kept or revealed, affect characters in the story? Do you agree with the reasons they were withheld from others? If you have ever concealed a major truth from a loved one, do you now regret it or feel it was justified?

9. Army Private Ian Downing, whom Vivian encounters at the café, first appeared in Kristina McMorris' debut novel, *Letters from Home*. If you were previously familiar with his character, how does his personality differ in *The Pieces We Keep*?

10. Who was your favorite character early in the book, and why? Did your opinion change as the story progressed? Who was your favorite character by the end?

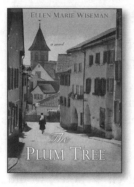

THE PLUM TREE

Ellen Marie Wiseman

A deeply moving and masterfully written story of human resilience and enduring love, *The Plum Tree* follows a young German woman through the chaos of World War II and its aftermath. "Bloom where you're planted," is the advice Christine Bölz receives from her beloved Oma. But seventeen-year-old domestic Christine knows there is a whole world waiting beyond her small German village. It's a world she's begun to glimpse through music, books—and through Isaac Bauerman, the cultured son of the wealthy Jewish family she works for. Yet the future she and Isaac dream of sharing faces greater challenges than their difference in stations. In the fall of 1938, Germany is changing rapidly under Hitler's regime. Anti-Jewish posters are everywhere, dissenting talk is silenced, and a new law forbids Christine from returning to her job—and from having any relationship with Isaac. In the months and years that follow, Christine will confront the Gestapo's wrath and the horrors of Dachau, desperate to be with the man she loves, to survive—and finally, to speak out. Set against the backdrop of the German homefront, this is an unforgettable novel of courage and resolve, of the inhumanity of war, and the heartbreak and hope left in its wake.

"In The Plum Tree, *Ellen Marie Wiseman boldly explores the complexities of the Holocaust. This novel is at times painful, but it is also a satisfying love story set against the backdrop of one of the most difficult times in human history."* —T. Greenwood, **author of** *Two Rivers*

"The meticulous hand-crafted detail and emotional intensity immersed me in Germany during its darkest hours and the ordeals its citizens had to face. A must-read for WWII fiction aficionados."—**Jenna Blum,** *The New York Times* **bestselling author of** *Those Who Save Us*

ABOUT THE AUTHOR: **Ellen Marie Wiseman** was born and raised in Three Mile Bay, a tiny hamlet in Northern New York. A first generation American, Ellen has traveled frequently to visit her family in Germany, where she fell in love with the country's history and culture. A mother of two, Ellen lives on the shores of Lake Ontario with her husband and three dogs.

January 2013 | Trade Paperback | Fiction | 304 pp | $15.00 | ISBN 9780758278432
Kensington Books | kensingtonbooks.com | ellenmariewiseman.com

CONVERSATION STARTERS

1. The first anti-Jewish poster Christine sees explains who is a Jew and who isn't, and forbids Jews to enter public places like banks and post offices. It is said that Hitler drew his first ideas about how to treat the Jews from blacks being denied civil rights in the South. What do you think are the differences? Why was the KKK kept in check while the Nazis were not?

2. Christine offers to hide Isaac before the Nazis take him and his family away. Would you have taken the opportunity to go with her, or would you have stayed with your family? Do you think Isaac's decision was based on loyalty to his parents and sister, or was it made because he thought they'd be okay since he had no idea how bad it was going to get?

3. The Nazis said they were going to "relocate" the Jews. What if this was happening where you live? How far would you be willing to go to protect your friends and neighbors? Would you risk your life or the lives of your children to save someone else?

4. How do you think Christine changed over the course of the novel? What about Isaac, Maria, Heinrich, and Karl? Even though siblings are raised together, sometimes they turn out differently. What differences do you see in Christine and Maria? Heinrich and Karl?

5. Discuss the significance of the plum tree. What does it symbolize, both as a pit when it's first planted and later, as a blossoming sapling at the end of the book?

6. When the Gestapo finds Isaac in Christine's attic, they spare the rest of her family out of respect for her father's military service. Do you think that would have happened, or do you think they would have shot her family or taken them all away?

7. Maria hates herself because the Russians raped her. She thinks no one will ever love her. When she finds out she is pregnant, she is devastated. Do you think she died by accident trying to get rid of the baby, or do you think she killed herself? What would you have done in her situation?

8. If Christine hadn't found out Isaac was alive, do you think she would have ended up with Jake?

THE RETURNED

Jason Mott

Harold and Lucille Hargrave's lives have been both joyful and sorrowful in the decades since their only son, Jacob, died tragically at his eighth birthday party in 1966. In their old age they've settled comfortably into life without him, their wounds tempered through the grace of time. Until one day Jacob mysteriously appears on their doorstep— flesh and blood, their sweet, precocious child, still eight years old.

All over the world, people's loved ones are returning from beyond. No one knows how or why, whether it's a miracle or a sign of the end. Not even Harold and Lucille can agree on whether the boy is real or a wondrous imitation, but one thing they know for sure: he's their son. As chaos erupts around the globe, the newly reunited Hargrave family finds itself at the center of a community on the brink of collapse, forced to navigate a mysterious new reality and a conflict that threatens to unravel the very meaning of what it is to be human.

"An extraordinary and beautifully realized novel. My spine is still shivering from the memory of this haunting story." —**Douglas Preston, #1 bestselling author of** *The Monster of Florence*

"In his exceptional debut novel, poet Mott brings drama, pathos, joy horror, and redemption to a riveting tale." —**Publishers Weekly, starred review**

"White-hot debut." —**Entertainment Weekly**

"This book offers a beautifully written and emotionally astute lens at our world done awry....Poet and debut author Mott has written a breathtaking novel that navigates emotional minefields with realism and grace." —**Kirkus, starred review**

ABOUT THE AUTHOR: **Jason Mott** holds a BA in fiction and an MFA in poetry and is the author of two poetry collections. His writing has appeared in numerous literary journals, and he was nominated for the 2009 Pushcart Prize. Jason lives in North Carolina. *The Returned* is currently being adapted for a network television drama series.

September 2013 | Hardcover | Fiction | 352 pp | $24.95 | ISBN 9780778315339
Harlequin MIRA | harlequin.com | jasonmottauthor.com

CONVERSATION STARTERS

1. Questions arise as to whether the Returned are miracles from God, or harbingers of the Devil. What was your initial reaction? Did it change over the course of the novel?

2. If possible, would you choose to call back a deceased loved one? Would you settle for their being somewhat altered, albeit "a copy" of what they were in life?

3. In the beginning of the novel, Lucille says, "I don't know what they are. All I know is they're not like you and me. ... They're Devils. They've just come here to kill us, or tempt us. These are the end days. ..." However, after the return of Jacob, she embraces him fully as her son. Did this surprise you? Do you think that she showed a natural maternal instinct? Can you imagine a mother responding differently?

4. How does Agent Bellamy's reaction to his Returned mother differ from that of Lucille and Harold? Why does he hide her true identity from them?

5. In a real life instance of the Returned, do you imagine a government intervention like the one in Arcadia? Why or why not?

6. Fred Green is fiercely opposed to the presence of the Returned. Why? How much of his reaction has to do with the death of his wife? How do you think he would have reacted had she returned?

7. Jason Mott writes a very moving Author's Note at the end of the novel. Did his explanation of his feelings following his mother's death and its influence on his writing affect the way you perceived the story? In retrospect, in which parts of the book do Mott's personal reckonings seem to emerge most strongly?

8. A passage at the end of the novel reads: "All the while, Lucille had never believed Jacob to be her son. But, all the while, Harold knew that he was. Maybe that's the way it was for everyone. Some folks locked the doors of their hearts when they lost someone. Others kept the doors and windows open, letting memory and love pass through freely. And maybe that was the way it was supposed to be, Harold thought." Discuss the idea expressed in this statement. Is *The Returned* a metaphor for the different ways we grieve?

THE ROUND HOUSE

Louise Erdrich

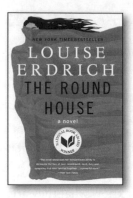

The Round House won the National Book Award for fiction.

One Sunday in the spring of 1988, a woman living on a reservation in North Dakota is attacked. The details of the crime are slow to surface as Geraldine Coutts is traumatized and reluctant to relive or reveal what happened, either to the police or to her husband, Bazil, and thirteen-year-old son, Joe. In one day, Joe's life is irrevocably transformed. He tries to heal his mother, but she will not leave her bed and slips into an abyss of solitude. Increasingly alone, Joe finds himself thrust prematurely into an adult world for which he is ill prepared.

While his father, who is a tribal judge, endeavors to wrest justice from a situation that defies his efforts, Joe becomes frustrated with the official investigation and sets out with his trusted friends, Cappy, Zack, and Angus, to get some answers of his own. Their quest takes them first to the Round House, a sacred space and place of worship for the Ojibwe. And this is only the beginning.

Written with undeniable urgency, and illuminating the harsh realities of contemporary life in a community where Ojibwe and white live uneasily together, The Round House is a brilliant and entertaining novel, a masterpiece of literary fiction. Louise Erdrich embraces tragedy, the comic, a spirit world very much present in the lives of her all-too-human characters, and a tale of injustice that is, unfortunately, an authentic reflection of what happens in our own world today.

ABOUT THE AUTHOR: **Louise Erdrich** is the author of thirteen novels as well as volumes of poetry, short stories, children's books, and a memoir of early motherhood. Her novel *Love Medicine* won the National Book Critics Circle Award. *The Last Report on the Miracles at Little No Horse* was a finalist for the National Book Award. Most recently, *The Plague of Doves* won the Anisfield-Wolf Book Award and was a finalist for the Pulitzer Prize. Louise Erdrich lives in Minnesota and is the owner of Birchbark Books, an independent bookstore.

October 2013 | Trade Paperback | Fiction | 368 pp | $15.99 | ISBN 9780062065254
Harper Perennial | harpercollins.com

CONVERSATION STARTERS

1. *The Round House* opens with the sentence: "Small trees had attacked my parents' house at the foundation." How do these words relate to the complete story that unfolds?

2. Though he is older as he narrates the story, Joe is just thirteen when the novel opens. What is the significance of his age? How does that impact the events that occur and his actions and reactions?

3. Describe Joe's family, and his relationship with his parents. In talking about his parents, Joe says, "I saw myself as different, though I didn't know how yet." Why, at thirteen, did he think this? Do you think the grown-up Joe narrating the story still believes this?

4. Joe's whole family is rocked by the attack on his mother. How does it affect the relationship between his mother and father, and between him and his mother? "My mother's job was to know everybody's secrets," Joe tells us. How does this knowledge empower Geraldine and how does it make her life more difficult?

5. What is the significance of the round house? What is the importance of the Ojibwe legends that are scattered through the novel? How do they reflect and deepen the main story? What can we learn from the old ways of people like the Ojibwe? Is Joe proud of his heritage? Discuss the connection between the natural and animal world and the tribe's spirituality.

6. Joe is inseparable from his three friends, especially his best friend, Cappy. Talk about their bond. How does their closeness influence unfolding events?

7. After the attack, Joe's mother, Geraldine, isn't sure exactly where it happened, whether it was technically on Reservation land or not. How does the legal relationship between the U.S. and the Ojibwe complicate the investigation? Why can't she lie to make it easier?

8. When Joe makes his fateful decision concerning his mother's attacker, he says it is about justice, not vengeance. What do you think?

9. What do you think about the status of Native Americans? Should we have reservations in modern America? How does the Reservation preserve their heritage and culture and how does it set them apart from their fellow Americans?

10. "The only thing that God can do, and does all the time, is to draw good from any evil situation," the priest advised Joe. What good does Joe—and also his family—draw from the events of the summer? What life lessons did Joe learn that summer of 1988?

THE SANDCASTLE GIRLS

Chris Bohjalian

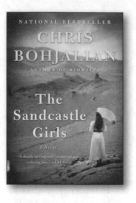

When Elizabeth Endicott arrives in Aleppo, Syria, she has a diploma from Mount Holyoke, a crash course in nursing, and only the most basic grasp of the Armenian language. It's 1915, and Elizabeth has volunteered to help deliver food and medical aid to refugees of the Armenian Genocide during the First World War. There she meets Armen, a young Armenian engineer who has already lost his wife and infant daughter. After leaving Aleppo and traveling into Egypt to join the British Army, he begins to write Elizabeth letters, realizing that he has fallen in love with the wealthy young American.

Years later, their American granddaughter, Laura, embarks on a journey back through her family's history, uncovering a story of love, loss—and a wrenching secret that has been buried for generations.

"A deeply moving story of survival and enduring love." —*USA Today*

"Bohjalian deftly weaves the many threads of this story back and forth, from past to present, from abuse to humanity, from devastation to redemption. . . . Utterly riveting." —*The Washington Post*

"Chris Bohjalian is at his very finest in this searing story of love and war. I was mesmerized from page one. Bravo!" —**Paula McLain, author of** *The Paris Wife*

"Bohjalian—the grandson of Armenian survivors—pours passion, pride, and sadness into his tale of ethnic destruction and endurance." —*Entertainment Weekly*

ABOUT THE AUTHOR: **Chris Bohjalian** is the critically acclaimed author of sixteen books, including *The New York Times* bestsellers *Skeletons at the Feast*, *The Double Bind*, and *Midwives*. His novel *Midwives* was a number one *New York Times* bestseller and a selection of Oprah's Book Club. Three of his novels have become movies (*Secrets of Eden*, *Midwives*, and *Past the Bleachers*). He lives in Vermont with his wife and daughter.

April 2013 | Trade Paperback | Fiction | 320 pp | $15.95 | ISBN 9780307743916
Vintage | randomhouse.com | chrisbohjalian.com

CONVERSATION STARTERS

1. Before reading *The Sandcastle Girls,* what did you know about the Armenian genocide? How does this history broaden your understanding of current events in the regions surrounding Armenia?

2. What lies at the heart of Armen and Elizabeth's attraction to each other, despite their seemingly different backgrounds? What gives their love the strength to transcend distance and danger?

3. The novel includes characters such as Dr. Akcam, Helmut, and Orhan, who take great risks opposing the atrocities committed by their superiors; Bohjalian does not cast the "enemy" as uniformly evil. What do these characters tell us about the process of resistance? What separates them from the others, who become capable of horrific, dehumanizing acts?

4. Why was it important for The Sandcastle Girls to be told primarily from the point of view of a woman? How was your reading affected by the knowledge that the author is a man?

5. When Laura describes the music of her 1960s youth, her steamy relationship with Berk, her belly-dancing aunt, and other cultural memories, what is she saying about the American experience of immigration and assimilation? Culturally, what did her grandfather sacrifice in order to gain security and prosperity in America?

6. Does Ryan Martin use his power effectively? How does Elizabeth gain power in a time period and culture that was marked by the oppression of women?

7. The vivid scenes of Gallipoli bring to life the global nature of war over the past century. As Armen fights alongside Australians, what do we learn about the power and the vulnerabilities of multinational forces? What did it mean for his fellow soldiers to fight for a cause so far removed from their own homelands, and for his own countrymen to rely on the mercy of outsiders?

8. As she tries to explain why so few people are aware of the Armenian genocide, Laura cites the fact that the victims perished in a remote desert. The novel also describes the problem of trying to document the atrocities using the cumbersome photography equipment of the day. Will the Information Age spell the end of such cover-ups? For future generations, will genocide be unimaginable?

SOMEONE ELSE'S LOVE STORY

Joshilyn Jackson

Someone Else's Love Story is beloved and highly acclaimed *New York Times* bestselling author Joshilyn Jackson's funny, charming, and poignant novel about science and miracles, secrets and truths, faith and forgiveness; about falling in love, and learning that things aren't always what they seem—or what we hope they will be.

Shandi Pierce is juggling finishing college, raising her delightful three-year-old genius son Nathan, aka Natty Bumppo, and keeping the peace between her eternally warring, long-divorced parents. She's got enough complications without getting caught in the middle of a stick-up and falling in love with William Ashe, who willingly steps between the robber and her son.

Shandi doesn't know that her blond god Thor has his own complications. When he looked down the barrel of that gun he believed it was destiny: It's been one year to the day since a tragic act of physics shattered his world. But William doesn't define destiny the way others do. A brilliant geneticist who believes in facts and numbers, destiny to him is about choice. Now, he and Shandi are about to meet their so-called destinies head on, making choices that will reveal unexpected truths about love, life, and the world they think they know.

*"A story that is never predictable and is awash in bittersweet love, regret and the promise of what could be. A surprising novel, both graceful and tender." —***Kirkus Review**

About the Author: *The New York Times* bestselling novelist **Joshilyn Jackson** lives in Decatur, Georgia with her husband, Scott, their two children. She is the author of five novels: *Gods in Alabama, Between, Georgia, The Girl Who Stopped Swimming, Backseat Saints,* and *A Grown-Up Kind of Pretty.* Her books have been translated into a dozen languages, won SIBA's novel of the year, twice been a #1 Book Sense Pick, twice won Georgia Author of the Year, and twice been shortlisted for the Townsend prize.

November 2013 | Hardcover | Fiction | 352 pp | $26.99 | ISBN 9780062105653
William Morrow | harpercollins.com | joshilynjackson.com

CONVERSATION STARTERS

1. What does the title tell you about the story? What do we learn from the first line? How does the book's opening set the stage for the events that follow?

2. "That afternoon in the Circle K, I deserved to know, right off, that I had landed bang in the middle of a love story. Especially since it wasn't—it isn't--- it could never be, my own." Why could this story never be Shandi's? If it's not hers, than whose love story is it?

3. Everyone sees William as a hero for his acts during the robbery. How does William answer this? Would you call it brave? Why did Shandi have such faith that William would save them?

4. Destiny and choice are major themes in the novel. What does destiny mean to William? What about Shandi?

5. Shandi and Walcott have known each other forever. Discuss their relationship. How is it transformed? Why do we often miss the obvious in our lives?

6. How do the religious references sprinkled through the story--Natty's virgin birth for example--add a deeper level of flavor and meaning to the book?

7. Why is William angry with Bridget and not her "imaginary God"? When bad things happen most people blame God. Why? Why doesn't William?

8. How does their meeting change both William and Shandi? Would you call their meeting fate or destiny or maybe a miracle? "It isn't every day he meets a girl who killed a miracle," William thinks when he agrees to help Shandi. Why does her having "killed" a miracle so intrigue him?

9. How do each of these characters' certainties and beliefs change when they are confronted by unexpected circumstances--the robbery, the fireworks, the DNA results, meeting Natty's father for example?

10. The possibility of goodness and forgiveness are also themes in the book. Talk about how they are demonstrated in various characters' lives and experiences.

11. How many different kinds of love stories are in the book? How do they all intertwine?

12. Were you surprised at the ending? Was it exactly what should happen for all the characters?

A SPEAR OF SUMMER GRASS

Deanna Raybourn

Kenya, 1923

Fairlight is the crumbling, sun-bleached skeleton of a faded African dream, a world where dissolute expats are bolstered by gin and jazz records, cigarettes and safaris. As mistress of this wasted estate, Delilah falls into the decadent pleasures of society.

Against the frivolity of her peers, Ryder White stands in sharp contrast. As foreign to Delilah as Africa, Ryder becomes her guide to the complex beauty of this unknown world. Giraffes, buffalo, lions, and elephants roam the shores of Lake Wanyama amid swirls of red dust. Here, life is lush and teeming—yet fleeting and often cheap.

Amidst the wonders—and dangers—of Africa, Delilah awakes to a land out of all proportion: extremes of heat, darkness, beauty, and joy that cut to her very heart. Only when this sacred place is profaned by bloodshed does Delilah discover what is truly worth fighting for—and what she can no longer live without.

"From sweetly touching moments requiring tissues to hot-blooded hunts for prey of both two- and four-legged varieties, this book elicits the widest range of emotions, and does it with style." —Library Journal, starred review

"Part romance, part travelogue, part murder mystery, featuring characters whose paths cross in the wilds of Africa. . . . An exotic journey of redemption." —*Kirkus*

ABOUT THE AUTHOR: *The New York Times* bestselling author **Deanna Raybourn** graduated from the University of Texas at San Antonio. She taught high school English for three years in San Antonio before leaving education to pursue a career as a novelist. Deanna makes her home in Virginia, where she lives with her husband and daughter and is hard at work on her next novel.

May 2013 | Trade Paperback | Fiction | 384 pp | $15.95 | ISBN 9780778314394
Harlequin MIRA | harlequin.com | deannaraybourn.com

CONVERSATION STARTERS

1. Delilah Drummond is a unique and not always likable heroine. How do the different characters in the book view her—as a friend or adversary? What was your reaction to her? How does Delilah change over the course of the book?

2. Ryder White is a larger-than-life character. What traits make him appealing?

3. How does the political climate of colonial Kenya influence the characters and their response to their environment? How does Dodo display attitudes typical of the colonial English? In contrast, the Farradays are representative of a particular type of scandalous settler notorious in Kenya between the 1920s and 1950s. How do you think each of these characters views Africa?

4. Gideon and his younger brother, Moses, both touch something within Delilah. What does this relationship seem to fulfill for each of them? Delilah makes a tremendous sacrifice for Gideon. Why? Was she right to do it?

5. Delilah is very comfortable with her sexuality and with the effect she has on men. How do sexual relationships drive the action of the book? How is Delilah's sexual relationship with Kit different from that with Ryder? How does Dodo's experience with sex change her plans?

6. Africa is as much a character in the book as any of the people. How does Africa itself play a role in the story?

7. Ryder makes tremendous sacrifices to keep Delilah in Africa. Was he right to do so?

8. What is Delilah and Ryder's potential for a happy ending?

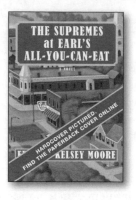

THE SUPREMES AT EARL'S ALL-YOU-CAN-EAT

Edward Kelsey Moore

A big-hearted debut novel about three devoted friends in a small Southern Indiana town who meet every Sunday at Earl's diner to support one another through thick and thin.

Earl's All-You-Can-Eat diner is home away from home for Odette, Claudine, and Barbara Jean. Dubbed "the Supremes" by high school pals in the tumultuous 1960s, they have weathered life's storms together for the next four decades. Now, during their most challenging year yet, dutiful, proud, and talented Clarice must struggle to keep up appearances as she deals with her husband's humiliating infidelities. Beautiful, fragile Barbara Jean is rocked by the tragic reverberations of a youthful love affair. And fearless Odette engages in the most terrifying battle of her life while contending with the idea that she has inherited more than her broad frame from her notorious mother, Dora. With wit and love, style and sublime talent, Edward Kelsey Moore brings together four intertwined love stories, three devoted allies, and two sprightly earthbound spirits in a novel you will never forget.

"*Moore knows how to write a terrific, complex, believable, and always intriguing story.*" —**Zetta Brown, *The New York Journal of Books***

"*Moore is a demonstrative storyteller and credits youthful eavesdropping for inspiring this multifaceted novel. Comparisons to* The Help *and* Fried Green Tomatoes at the Whistle Stop Cafe *are inevitable, but Moore's take on this rowdy troupe of outspoken, lovable women has its own distinctive pluck.*" —**Publishers Weekly**

"*A gripping novel that weaves together the lives of three remarkable women, and does so with flair, wit, and tremendous heart.*" —**Carolina De Robertis, author of *Perla* and *The Invisible Mountain***

About the Author: **Edward Kelsey Moore** lives in Chicago, where he has enjoyed a long career as a cellist. His short fiction has appeared in several literary magazines. His short story "Grandma and the Elusive Fifth Crucifix" was selected as an audience favorite on National Public Radio's *Stories on Stage* series.

January 2014 | Trade Paperback | Fiction | 320 pp | $15.00 | ISBN 9780307950437
Vintage | randomhouse.com | edwardkelseymoore.com

CONVERSATION STARTERS

1. Odette was born in a sycamore tree. Barbara Jean was born on the wrong side of the tracks. Clarice was the first black baby to be born in an all-white hospital. How do the circumstances of each woman's birth shape her choices as an adult? Their interactions with one another? Their relationships with their husbands?

2. Odette, Clarice, and Barbara Jean are best friends, but they're quite different. What is a defining moment in each of their lives?

3. The chapters alternate between Odette's voice and an omniscient third-person narrator. What is the effect of this in storytelling? Why does Moore choose Odette as a narrator rather than Clarice or Barbara Jean?

4. One of Dora Jackson's beliefs is that "what we call miracles is just what's supposed to happen. We either go with it or stand in its way." What seemingly miraculous events occur in the novel, and why do some characters choose to "go with it" and others "stand in [their] way"?

5. Earl's All-You-Can-Eat is the first black-owned restaurant in Plainview, Indiana. What role does place play in the novel, and how does the diner shape the lives of the main characters?

6. The Supremes grew up in tumultuous times. How was each one of them affected by the major social changes for African Americans, as well as for women, that occurred over the course of their lives?

7. Why does Clarice decide not to move back in with Richmond, even after he feels they've patched things up? What other changes do you see in Clarice after her separation from her husband, specifically in her relationship with music and religion? Do you think she will follow her dream as a musician?

8. Whether alive or dead (or a ghost), the mothers of the Supremes play a major role in their daughters' lives. As the Supremes grow older, how do their mothers continue to exert an influence on their adult lives? Who is hurt most by it? Who is helped by it? Who is most like her mother as she gets older?

9. Odette, Clarice, and Barbara Jean each attend three very different churches. In what ways did growing up in these particular churches help to shape them into the women they ultimately became?

THE SWEETEST HALLELUJAH

Elaine Hussey

An unforgettable story of two courageous women brought together by one extraordinary little girl. Betty Jewel Hughes was once the hottest black jazz singer in Memphis. But when she finds herself pregnant and alone, she gives up her dream of being a star to raise her beautiful daughter, Billie, in Shakerag, Mississippi. Now, ten years later, in 1955, Betty Jewel is dying of cancer and looking for someone to care for Billie when she's gone. With no one she can count on, Betty Jewel does the unthinkable: she takes out a want ad seeking a loving mother for her daughter.

Meanwhile, on the other side of town, recently widowed Cassie Malone is an outspoken housewife insulated by her wealth and privileged white society. Working part-time at a newspaper, she is drawn to Betty Jewel through her mysterious ad. With racial tension in the South brewing, the women forge a bond as deep as it is forbidden. But neither woman could have imagined the gifts they would find in each other, and in the sweet young girl they both love with all their hearts. Deeply moving and richly evocative, *The Sweetest Hallelujah* is a remarkable tale about finding hope in a time of turmoil, and about the transcendent and transformative power of friendship.

"A certain fairy-tale realism—similar to that of The Help, *which this book will inevitably be compared to—makes the concept both believable and entertaining. . . . An endearing and emotionally satisfying exploration of race, family and friendship in trying times." —**Kirkus Reviews***

ABOUT THE AUTHOR: **Elaine Hussey** is a writer, actress, and musician who likes to describe herself as "southern to the bone." She lives in Mississippi, where her love of blues and admiration for the unsung heroes of her state's history served as inspiration for *The Sweetest Hallelujah*.

August 2013 | Trade Paperback | Fiction | 352 pp | $15.95 | ISBN 9780778315193
Harlequin MIRA | halequin.com | elainehussey.com

CONVERSATION STARTERS

1. Discuss how the themes of sin and redemption play out in the lives of Betty Jewel and Cassie. In what ways does Cassie save Betty Jewel and vice versa?

2. What do you think of Cassie's decision to adopt Billie? Is it dangerous? Selfless? What does it say about Cassie's character, about her friendship with Betty Jewel, and about her marriage to Joe? Would you have made the same choice? Why or why not?

3. Discuss the role of family in the book. In what ways does familial responsibility drive the actions of the characters? Do you agree or disagree with the line "Family is family no matter what"? Why or why not?

4. *"The Sweetest Hallelujah"* features a cast of strong female characters: Betty Jewel, Cassie, Billie, Queen, Fay Dean, Sudie and Merry Lynn. Discuss each of their roles in the story and how they drive the narrative forward. Which of the characters do you relate to the most and why? Do you have a favorite?

5. The novel is told in alternating perspectives between Cassie, Betty Jewel and Billie. How does this affect how you read/understand the book? What are the advantages and disadvantages of multi-perspective storytelling?

6. History plays a particularly important role in *"The Sweetest Hallelujah."* In what ways does the setting and period (Mississippi in the summer of 1955) impact the story? How would the story have been different if it had been set in the present?

7. Discuss Billie's journey in the story and her relationship to Betty Jewel, Queen, Saint, Cassie, and Mike Malone. How does each of these characters impact Billie's life? How do you think her life will play out after the last page of the book has been turned?

8. Discuss the role of Dead Alice in the story. What does her presence signify, and how does it change throughout the book?

9. Betty Jewel, the Saint, and Joe are all musicians. There are song lyrics referenced throughout the book, and the gentle sound of the blues is present at every turn. Discuss the significance of blues and music in the story?

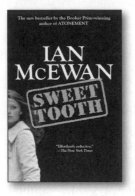

SWEET TOOTH

Ian McEwan

One of the Best Books of the Year
The New York Times, San Francisco Chronicle, Seattle Times

Cambridge student Serena Frome's beauty and intelligence make her the ideal recruit for M15. The year is 1972. The Cold War is far from over. England's legendary intelligence agency is determined to manipulate the cultural conversation by funding writers whose politics align with those of the government. The operation is code named "Sweet Tooth." Serena, a compulsive reader of novels, is the perfect candidate to infiltrate the literary circle of a promising young writer named Tom Haley. At first, she loves the stories. Then she begins to love the man. How long can she conceal her undercover life? To answer that question, Serena must abandon the first rule of espionage: trust no one.

*"A subtly and sweetly subversive novel [that is a] masterful manipulation of the relationship(s) between fiction and truth . . . Britain's foremost living novelist has written a book as drily funny as it is thoughtful." —***Kirkus Reviews,** *starred review*

*"McEwan's most stylish and personal book to date . . . The year's most intensely enjoyable novel." —***The Daily Beast**

*"A wisecracking thriller hightailing between love and betrayal, with serious counter-espionage credentials thrown in . . . This is ultimately a book about writing, wordplay and knowingness." —***The Telegraph**

About the Author: **Ian McEwan** is the bestselling author of fourteen books, including the novels *Solar; On Chesil Beach; Saturday; Atonement,* winner of the National Book Critics Circle Award and the W. H. Smith Literary Award; *The Comfort of Strangers* and *Black Dogs,* both shortlisted for the Booker Prize; *Amsterdam,* winner of the Booker Prize; and *The Child in Time,* winner of the Whitbread Award; as well as the story collections *First Love, Last Rites,* winner of the Somerset Maugham Award, and *In Between the Sheets.* He lives in England.

July 2013 | Trade Paperback | Fiction | 400 pp | $15.95 | ISBN 9780345803450
Anchor | randomhouse.com | ianmcewan.com

CONVERSATION STARTERS

1. Why do you believe that the author chose to set a contemporary novel in the England of the 1970s during the lingering Cold War?

2. McEwan chooses to employ a female protagonist. Is she convincing? What surprises you about her character?

3. Is *Sweet Tooth* truly a spy novel? How does it fulfill or defy your expectations of this genre? In addition to portraying spying for political purposes, how else is the theme of spying treated? Who in the novel is a spy? Who is spied on and for what purpose?

4. Who is betrayed or deceived in the novel? How do they react to these deceptions or betrayals?

5. How does *Sweet Tooth* compare to McEwan's 1990 spy novel *The Innocent*? What do the two novels share in common?

6. In Chapter 8, Serena says that "Haley had got under [her] skin, and [she] wondered if he was one of those necessary men"—an "impermissible" thought, she adds. What does she mean by this? Why might this characterization of Haley be considered "impermissible"?

7. Excerpts from Haley's short stories are peppered throughout the novel. What impact does McEwan's use of metafiction—described by *The Guardian*'s Julie Myerson as a Russian doll effect—have on the reader? How are the major themes of the novel mirrored—or otherwise contradicted—in Haley's stories?

8. Serena accuses Haley of "easy nihilism". What does she mean by this? Does Haley's own world-view, in fact, seem consistent with the view touted in his apocalyptic novel? Do Serena's observations about "easy nihilism" affect your reaction of her actions throughout the novel?

9. Why doesn't Serena tell Tom about her work? Could she have told him? Should she have? Consider Tom's account of his discovery of Serena's role in Operation Sweet Tooth. What does her dilemma and Tom's reaction seem to indicate about ethics and morality? Are the views evinced by each character consistent with or in opposition to one another?

10. What view of religion and faith is presented in the novel? How does the conclusion of the book change your view or perception of the preceding events and of the characters involved? Of the book's overall messages and themes?

TELEGRAPH AVENUE

Michael Chabon

As the summer of 2004 draws to a close, Archy Stallings and Nat Jaffe are still hanging in there—longtime friends, bandmates, and co-regents of Brokeland Records, a kingdom of used vinyl located in the borderlands of Berkeley and Oakland. Their wives, Gwen Shanks and Aviva Roth-Jaffe, are the Berkeley Birth Partners, a pair of semi-legendary midwives who have welcomed more than a thousand newly minted citizens into the dented utopia at whose heart—half tavern, half temple—stands Brokeland.

When ex–NFL quarterback Gibson Goode, the fifth-richest black man in America, announces plans to build his latest Dogpile megastore on a nearby stretch of Telegraph Avenue, Nat and Archy fear it means certain doom for their vulnerable little enterprise. Meanwhile, Aviva and Gwen also find themselves caught up in a battle for their professional existence, one that tests the limits of their friendship. Adding another layer of complications to the couples' already tangled lives is the surprise appearance of Titus Joyner, the teenage son Archy has never acknowledged and the love of fifteen-year-old Julius Jaffe's life.

"An amazingly rich, emotionally detailed story . . . [Chabon's] people become so real to us, their problems so palpably netted in the author's buoyant, expressionistic prose, that the novel gradually becomes a genuinely immersive experience." —**Michiko Kakutani,** *The New York Times*

"Astounding. . . . [A] huge-hearted, funny, improbably hip book." —**John Freeman,** *The Boston Globe*

About the Author: **Michael Chabon** is the bestselling and Pulitzer Prize-winning author of *The Mysteries of Pittsburgh, Wonder Boys, The Amazing Adventures of Kavalier & Clay, Summerland* (a novel for children), *The Final Solution, The Yiddish Policemen's Union,* and *Gentlemen of the Road,* as well as the short story collections *A Model World* and *Werewolves in Their Youth* and the essay collections *Maps and Legends* and *Manhood for Amateurs.* He is the chairman of the board of the MacDowell Colony. He lives in Berkeley, California, with his wife, the novelist Ayelet Waldman, and their children.

September 2013 | Trade Paperback | Fiction | 496 pp | $16.99 | ISBN 9780061493355
Harper Perennial | harpercollins.com | michaelchabon.com

CONVERSATION STARTERS

1. There are many different variations on father-and-son relationships—both real and makeshift—explored in the novel. What might the author be trying to convey through these complicated liaisons?

2. Like her husband, Archy, Gwen is African American, but of a decidedly different social class, upbringing, and education. How do these differences affect her marriage, as well as her position in this close-knit Oakland community—both in her own view and in the view of others?

3. As the legendary Berkeley Birth Partners, Gwen Shanks and Aviva Roth-Jaffe have worked together for many years, and their husbands are business partners as well. Beyond their professional lives, what sense do you get of the friendship between these two women? How does the crisis that confronts their business bring out the best and/or worst in their pairing?

4. Telegraph Avenue, the real-life Bay Area street at the center of the story, is described as "the ragged fault where the urban plates of Berkeley and Oakland subducted." How do the conflicting cultures of upper-middle-class Berkeley and working-class Oakland clash in the novel?

5. When a home birth goes awry, the midwife Gwen goes ballistic when faced with criticism from an obstetrician at the hospital. The emotional outburst severely jeopardizes her career. Do you think she is justified in her reaction, or should she have tempered her response?

6. *Telegraph Avenue* is set during the summer of 2004 in Oakland, California. Do this time and place have special bearing on the events of the novel, or could the story take place in a different or more ambiguous setting?

7. Some of the characters in the novel seem to be holding onto the past, as evidenced by their love of vinyl records and 1970s "Blaxploitation" martial arts films. How do you think this attachment to the past affects the characters' grasp on their present realities?

8. Archy Stallings makes some questionable choices in his dealings with his wife, Gwen, his son, Titus, his partner, Nat, and his business rival, Gibson Goode. Do you find him a sympathetic character?

9. How would you assess the relationship between Julius and Titus? Is it a genuine friendship for both of them?

10. The novel is filled with colorful, eccentric characters. Which did you feel were the most arresting? The most real? Why?

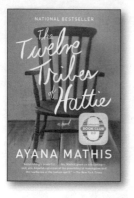

THE TWELVE TRIBES OF HATTIE

Ayana Mathis

An Oprah's Book Club 2.0 Selection

In 1923, against the backdrop of the Great Migration, fifteen-year-old Hattie Shepherd flees Georgia and heads north. Full of hope, she settles in Philadelphia to build a better life. Instead she marries a man who will bring her nothing but disappointment, and watches helplessly as her firstborn twins are lost to an illness that a few pennies could have prevented. Hattie gives birth to nine more children, whom she raises with grit, mettle, and not an ounce of the tenderness they crave. She vows to prepare them to meet a world that will not be kind. Their lives, captured here in twelve luminous threads, tell the story of a mother's monumental courage—and the driving force of the American dream.

"The opening pages of Ayana's debut took my breath away. I can't remember when I read anything that moved me in quite this way, besides the work of Toni Morrison." —**Oprah Winfrey**

"Lush yet deliberate . . . elegant and sure . . . a complex and deeply humane story of a mother's ferocious love and failures at loving...In the vivid specificity of Mathis's tale, she is telling a universal story, and it is profoundly consoling." —**Laura Collins-Hughes, *The Boston Globe***

"Mathis never loses touch with the geography and the changing national culture through which her characters move. The Twelve Tribes of Hattie is infused with African Americans' conflicted attitudes about the North and the South during the Great Migration. . . . In the long family arc that Mathis describes, the painful life of one remarkably resilient woman is placed against the hopes and struggles of millions of African Americans who held this nation to its promise. . . . One of the best [novels] of 2012." —**Ron Charles, *The Washington Post***

About the Author: **Ayana Mathis** is a graduate of the Iowa Writers' Workshop and is a recipient of the Michener-Copernicus Fellowship. *The Twelve Tribes of Hattie* is her first novel. Originally from Philadelphia, she lives in Brooklyn.

October 2013 | Trade Paperback | Fiction | 320 pp | $15.00 | ISBN 9780307949707
Vintage | randomhouse.com | ayanamathis.com

CONVERSATION STARTERS

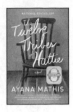

1. Hattie is, by any measure, a complicated, difficult woman. Did you love her, hate her, find it difficult to have sympathy for her? Is she a good mother? Why or why not?

2. In one of the novel's most dramatic and revealing chapters, Hattie leaves August with the older children and escapes with baby Ruthie (then called Margaret) and her lover, Lawrence. How did this make you feel? Were you hoping she would stay with Lawrence or go back to August and the children?

3. What do you learn in the chapter called "Ruthie" about August as a husband? As a father? As a man?

4. Does August change throughout the course of the novel? Do you feel differently about him at the novel's end than at the beginning?

5. Discuss the disagreement between Hattie and August in the chapter "Ruthie" about Cassie learning to play piano. Who is right? What kind of marriage do Hattie and August have?

6. Discuss the scene in which Pearl and Benny are interrupted during their picnic by a group of white men. How did you feel about Benny's choices? Does Pearl have a right to be angry? What do you think you would have done in these circumstances?

7. Reread the anguished scene in which Hattie and August give Ella to Marion and Benny. August tells Hattie, "We had that pain . . . and we'll have this too." Did they do the right thing? Was this chapter tragic? Hopeful?

8. Why does Franklin throw his letter to Sissy into the bay? Is this an act of cowardice, or could it be read as heroism?

9. In one of the novel's climactic moments, Hattie and Lawrence bump into each other in a department store, and she discovers that Lawrence is romantically entangled with her daughter Bell. Why does Bell seduce Lawrence? What does she hope to achieve? What, if anything, does she learn about herself after her mother discovers her affair?

10. Why does Hattie refuse to let Sala take the mercy seat?

11. Reread the novel's final paragraph. Is this a happy ending or a heartbreaking one? Resigned, or hopeful? Did you feel differently about Hattie in the novel's last lines? Has she changed?

VISIT SUNNY CHERNOBYL

And Other Adventures in the World's Most Polluted Places

Andrew Blackwell

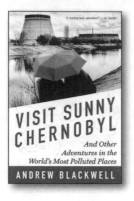

For most of us, traveling means visiting the most beautiful places on Earth—Paris, the Taj Mahal, the Grand Canyon. It's rare to book a plane ticket to visit the lifeless moonscape of Canada's oil sand strip mines, or to set sail for the Great Pacific Garbage Patch. But in *Visit Sunny Chernobyl,* Andrew Blackwell embraces a different kind of travel, taking a jaunt through the most gruesomely polluted places on Earth.

Visit Sunny Chernobyl fuses immersive first-person reporting with satire and analysis, making the case that it's time to start appreciating our planet as-is—not as we wish it to be. Equal parts travelogue, expose environmental memoir, and faux guidebook, Blackwell careens through a rogue's gallery of environmental disaster areas in search of the worst the world has to offer—and approaches a deeper understanding of what's really happening to our planet in the process.

"A darkly comic romp."—**Elizabeth Kolbert,** *The New Yorker*

"An environmentalist book that avoids the usual hyperventilation, upending stubborn myths with prosaic facts . . . Blackwell is a smart and often funny writer."—*The Wall Street Journal*

"Witty and disturbing . . . Call this the anti-guide book."—***New York Post*** **"Required Reading"**

ABOUT THE AUTHOR: **Andrew Blackwell** is a journalist and filmmaker. He is a 2011 Fellow in Nonfiction Literature from the New York Foundation of the Arts. *Visit Sunny Chernobyl* is his first book. He lives in New York City.

May 2013 | Trade Paperback | Nonfiction | 320 pp | $15.99 | ISBN 9781623360269
Rodale Books | rodaleinc.com | visitsunnychernobyl.com

CONVERSATION STARTERS

1. Before reading *Visit Sunny Chernobyl*, what did you know about polluted places around the world? Have you ever known anyone who purposely visited a less-than-desirable locale as an adventure or vacation?

2. Blackwell describes touring the ghost city of Pripyat near the Chernobyl reactor. How did his tour change your perception of this notorious nuclear "ground zero"?

3. The sites in the book that directly relate to oil consumption and production—the refineries of Port Arthur, Texas and the oil sands in Canada—give a glimpse at the sheer scope of the energy industry and what it must do to meet global demand. Considering that almost everyone in the developed world drives a car, how do you feel about your own role in how these sites are treated?

4. Thinking about the Great Pacific Garbage Patch, do you know where your trash goes after it's picked up?

5. As the author says, India considers its rivers to be holy, and yet we see in the book that the Yamuna and Ganges rivers are among the most polluted in the world. How do you reconcile that? Is there a link to a more global attitude in the way the entire world considers the planet sacred, yet continues to destroy it?

6. Soy farming—providing food and jobs to a large number of people—is the primary reason we see the deforested Amazonian landscapes in the book. It's also the reason for the condition of many other destinations in *Visit Sunny Chernobyl*. Should planet come before people?

7. In general, when people book a vacation, they want to travel somewhere beautiful. Do you think this is a case of "beauty is in the eye of the beholder," or have you ever found beauty in ruined places or things?

8. One of the themes of *Visit Sunny Chernobyl* is learning to appreciate the planet the way it is, not the way we think it should be. Do you agree or disagree?

9. Has *Visit Sunny Chernobyl* changed your outlook on the current state of our planet, or how we view it from the safety of clean homes and perks like flushing toilets?

10. Would you ever visit any of the locations in *Visit Sunny Chernobyl*? Which ones and why?

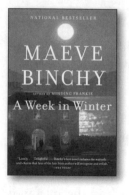

A WEEK IN WINTER

Maeve Binchy

Stoneybridge is a small town on the west coast of Ireland where all the families know one another. When Chicky Starr decides to take an old, decaying mansion set high on the cliffs overlooking the wind-swept Atlantic Ocean and turn it into a restful place for a holiday by the sea, everyone thinks she is crazy. Helped by Rigger (a bad boy turned good who is handy around the house) and Orla, her niece (a whiz at business), Chicky is finally ready to welcome the first guests to Stone House's big warm kitchen, log fires, and understated elegant bedrooms. John, the American movie star, thinks he has arrived incognito; Winnie and Lillian are forced into taking a holiday together; Nicola and Henry, husband and wife, have been shaken by seeing too much death practicing medicine; Anders hates his father's business, but has a real talent for music; Miss Nell Howe, a retired schoolteacher, criticizes everything and leaves a day early, much to everyone's relief; the Walls are disappointed to have won this second-prize holiday in a contest where first prize was Paris; and Freda, the librarian, is afraid of her own psychic visions.

"Fittingly, this posthumously published work by Ireland's beloved lady of letters is itself a love letter to her homeland. . . . Binchy offers a final chance to enjoy her winning characters and the charm of Irish culture. . . . Reading this novel is like ducking out of a cold rain into a fire-warmed pub filled with laughter." —**People**

ABOUT THE AUTHOR: **Maeve Binchy** was the author of five collections of short stories as well as twelve novels including *Circle of Friends, The Copper Beech, Tara Road, Evening Class* and *The Glass Lake.* Maeve Binchy died in July 2012 and is survived by her husband, the writer Gordon Snell.

January 2014 | Trade Paperback | Fiction | 336 pp | $14.95 | ISBN 9780307475503
Anchor | randomhouse.com | maevebinchy.com

CONVERSATION STARTERS

1. Why is Chicky attracted to Walter? Why does she defy her mother's doubts and admonitions about going to New York?

2. After Walter leaves, Chicky vows she will never go back to Stoneybridge. Is she motivated by pride and stubbornness or does her decision reflect realistic concerns about the reactions her return is likely to generate?

3. In Winnie and Lillian's antagonistic relationship, which woman initially has the upper hand and why? How does Teddy's behavior affect their opinions and interactions?

4. What does Anders's story convey about the difficulties of making a choice when one is faced with a conflict between duty and desire? How do his mother's and Erika's actions and advice, as well as his relationship with his father, influence him?

5. Nell Howe is the only guest unmoved by the charms of Stone House. What accounts for her resistance to the atmosphere at the inn and her critical opinions of her fellow guests? What do her conversations with Rigger and Carmel reveal about her and the reasons she is unable or unwilling to bond with other people? Does her stay at Stone House change her in any way?

6. Why does Freda try to ignore or repress the visions she has? How do they interfere with her everyday life and her hopes and plans for the future? Even without her special "feelings," is she foolish to embark on a love affair with Mark? Why does she decide to tell a "group of strangers" about her psychic powers? Reread the predictions she makes. Which of them do you think will come true?

7. Talk about how Binchy introduces each of the guests at Stone House. How does she pique your interest in them? Which character makes the strongest first impression? Which one takes the longest to get to know?

8. Anders tells himself, "Problems don't solve themselves neatly like that, due to a set of coincidences. Problems are solved by making decisions." Discuss how the various stories in *A Week in Winter* confirm or belie this observation.

9. Minor characters are an important part of *A Week in Winter*. What do Miss Queenie, Orla, Rigger, and Carmel contribute to the novel?

THE WEIGHT OF SMALL THINGS

Sherri Wood Emmons

From the acclaimed author of *Prayers and Lies* and *The Sometimes Daughter* comes an emotional, compelling, and ultimately uplifting novel that explores the fragility and resilience of love—and the decisions, large and small, that determine not just who we are, but who we want to be.

Corrie Philips has an enviable life—even if it's not quite the one she wanted. She enjoys working at her university alumni magazine, her house is beautiful, and her husband, Mark, is attentive, handsome, and wealthy. But after years of frustration and failed attempts, Corrie is desperate for a child—and haunted by the choices in her past.

A decade ago, just after college, Corrie's boyfriend Daniel left town, intent on saving the world even if it meant breaking Corrie's heart. Now he's returned, and despite her misgivings, Corrie feels drawn to him again. But the emotions that overwhelm her may put her marriage and her secure, stable life at risk. Faced with an unexpected choice, Corrie must unravel illusion from reality at last and weigh what she most needs against what her heart has always wanted.

"Emmons is undoubtedly a wonderful storyteller, and readers will be drawn to her characters and their situations. It will not be hard to lose yourself in the drama and readers will be able to relate to two women who evaluate the effects of past decisions in present life." —RT Book Reviews

ABOUT THE AUTHOR: **Sherri Wood Emmons**, a freelance writer and editor, is an Indiana Authors Award Finalist. She is a graduate of Earlham College and the University of Denver Publishing Institute. A mother of three, Sherri lives in Indiana with her husband, two fat beagles, and four spoiled cats.

April 2013 | Trade Paperback | Fiction | 400 pp | $15.00 | ISBN 9780758280435
Kensington Books | kensingtonbooks.com | sherriwoodemmons.com

CONVERSATION STARTERS

1. Corrie Philips seems to have an ideal life. Why can't she let go of the past and enjoy the present?

2. Is Corrie a sympathetic character? Why or why not?

3. Bob insists to Bryn that she tell Paul about her pregnancy. Do you think a man always has the right to know when his partner is pregnant? Are there times when it's okay to keep that information from him?

4. What responsibility, if any, does Corrie have for her mother's situation?

5. Corrie believes that her inability to conceive a baby is punishment for having had an abortion. What does your faith tradition teach about God's judgment? How does that apply to a woman who has terminated a pregnancy?

6. What role does Maya play in the story? How would the story be different without her presence?

7. Corrie accuses Daniel of trying to play God. Is that a fair assessment? Are Daniel's decisions reasonable ones?

8. Bob has taken his wayward wife back twice after her infidelities. Do you think a partner should be given a second chance after an affair?

9. Bryn's relationship with Paul began when she was his student. Is it ever okay for a teacher to be in a romantic relationship with a student? Why or why not?

10. Bob and Bryn begin their relationship very soon after his divorce. Is Bryn right to worry about being a rebound girlfriend? Can their relationship last?

11. Corrie and Daniel's relationship is renewed while she is married to Mark. Is the relationship doomed to fail? Why or why not?

12. What is the significance of the title, *The Weight of Small Things*?

WHISTLING PAST THE GRAVEYARD

Susan Crandall

The summer of 1963 begins like any other for nine-year-old Starla Claudelle. But Starla never dreams that she's about to embark on a journey that will change her life forever. When Starla's strict grandmother and guardian grounds her on the Fourth of July, Starla decides to run away from her Mississippi home and go to Nashville, to seek her mother who had abandoned her. On the road, Starla finds an unlikely ally in Eula—a lonely woman suffering loss and abuse. Through a series of unforeseen events, the black woman and the white girl band together on a path to self-discovery. As they travel, Starla's eyes are opened to the harsh realities of 1963 Southern segregation. Through her discussions with Eula, reconnection with both her parents, and a series of surprising misadventures, Starla begins to realize that having a life with the perfect family might look drastically different from how she dreamed it would.

"This coming-of-age story is a must for fans of Kathryn Stockett's The Help *or Harper Lee's classic* To Kill a Mockingbird." *—***Working Mother Magazine**

*"A luminous portrait of courage and the bonds of friendship, this coming of age story is as endearing and spirited as they come." —***Shape Magazine**

"It's not easy to keep such a young narrator convincing for more than 300 pages. . . . Readers will take to Starla and be caught up in her story." —**Mary Ellen Quinn,** *Booklist*

ABOUT THE AUTHOR: **Susan Crandall** is an award-winning women's fiction, suspense, romance, and mystery author. Her first book, *Back Roads*, won the RITA award for best first book, as well as two National Reader's Choice awards. She has released eight more critically acclaimed and award-winning novels. Susan lives in Indiana.

July 2013 | Hardcover | Fiction | 320 pp | $24.99 | ISBN 9781476707723
Gallery Books | simonandschuster.com | susancrandall.net

CONVERSATION STARTERS

1. By telling the story from Starla's point of view, we get to look at the South in 1963 through the eyes of a child. Why do you think the author chose a child narrator?

2. Secrets permeate the plot of the novel. As a child narrator, Starla has many secrets kept from her. Some secrets are to protect her, while others are simply too painful to share. Name a few of these secrets. Was the secret justified or would it have been better to reveal it earlier?

3. Eula claims that ultimately Wallace's downfall is his pride. Do you agree? Do you think that this is true or that Wallace is a victim of his circumstances? Do you sympathize with him at all?

4. After leaving Wallace behind and travelling with Starla, we see Eula beginning to find herself. Do you think that there's a specific moment when that happens?

5. Eula and Starla are both products of dysfunctional families. How different or similar are their coping mechanisms for dealing with their families? In what way do they influence each other as they grow stronger?

6. How do Starla's thoughts on religion evolve as she meets characters such as Eula and Miss Cyrena? Do you think she comes to a conclusion by the end of her journey?

7. In Miss Cyrena's neighborhood, Starla experiences first-hand the harsh reality of discrimination. How does her experience there change her and affect her character? She's even called a "polar bear." How does this affect her throughout the rest of the book?

8. Miss Cyrena claims that people never actually change, we just change our perception of them. To what degree do you think this is true? Does it apply to Wallace? Lulu? Mamie?

9. When they make a pie crust together, Eula warns Starla against "working the dough" too much. How do you think this is symbolic of Eula's philosophy in general? What does this teach Starla?

10. At the end of the story, Starla's father lives up to her dreams, but her mother disappoints her. How did you feel about each of them at the end of the story?

11. If this novel were a movie, who do you imagine would play Starla and Eula?

WILD
From Lost to Found on the Pacific Crest Trail
Cheryl Strayed

One of the Best Books of the Year
The Boston Globe, Entertainment Weekly,
NPR*, St. Louis Dispatch, Vogue*

Oprah's Book Club 2.0 Inaugural Selection

At twenty-two, Cheryl Strayed thought she had lost everything. In the wake of her mother's death, her family scattered and her own marriage was soon destroyed. Four years later, with nothing more to lose, she made the most impulsive decision of her life. With no experience or training, driven only by blind will, she would hike more than a thousand miles of the Pacific Crest Trail from the Mojave Desert through California and Oregon to Washington State—and she would do it alone. Told with suspense and style, sparkling with warmth and humor, *Wild* powerfully captures the terrors and pleasures of one young woman forging ahead against all odds on a journey that maddened, strengthened, and ultimately healed her.

"*Spectacular. . . . A literary and human triumph.*" —*The New York Times Book Review*

"*I was on the edge of my seat. . . . It is just a wild ride of a read . . . stimulating, thought-provoking, soul-enhancing.*" —**Oprah Winfrey**

"*Strayed's language is so vivid, sharp and compelling that you feel the heat of the desert, the frigid ice of the High Sierra, and the breathtaking power of one remarkable woman finding her way—and herself—one brave step at a time.*" —*People*

About the Author: **Cheryl Strayed** is the author of the critically-acclaimed novel *Torch*, which was a finalist for the Great Lakes Book Award and was selected by *The Oregonian* as one of the top ten books of 2006 by Pacific Northwest authors, and *Tiny Beautiful Things: Advice on Love and Life from Dear Sugar*. Her stories and essays have appeared in numerous magazines and journals, including *The New York Times Magazine, The Washington Post Magazine, Vogue, The Rumpus, Self, The Missouri Review,* and *The Sun*. Her essays have been included in the Pushcart Prize anthology and twice in *The Best American Essays*. She lives in Portland, Oregon.

March 2013 | Trade Paperback | Memoir | 336 pp | $15.95 | ISBN 9780307476074
Vintage | randomhouse.com | cherylstrayed.com

CONVERSATION STARTERS

1. Strayed is quite forthright in her description of her own transgressions, and while she's remorseful, she never seems ashamed. Is this a sign of strength or a character flaw?

2. Fear is a major theme in the book. Do you think Strayed was too afraid, or not afraid enough? When were you most afraid for her?

3. Strayed chose her own last name. Did she choose well? What did you think when you learned she had assigned this word to herself—that it was no coincidence?

4. On the trail, Strayed encounters mostly men. How does this work in her favor? What role does gender play when removed from the usual structure of society?

5. What does the reader learn from the horrific episode in which Strayed and her brother put down their mother's horse?

6. Strayed writes that the point of the Pacific Crest Trail (PCT) "had only to do with how it felt to be in the wild. With what it was like to walk for miles for no reason other than to witness the accumulation of trees and meadows, mountains and deserts, streams and rocks, rivers and grasses, sunrises and sunsets." How does this sensation help Strayed to find her way back into the world beyond the wilderness?

7. On her journey, Strayed carries several totems. What does the black feather mean to her? And the POW bracelet? Why does she find its loss symbolic?

8. Does the hike help Strayed get over Paul? If so, how? And if not, why?

9. How did being on the PCT on her mother's fiftieth birthday help Strayed to heal this wound?

10. What was it about Strayed that inspired the generosity of so many strangers on the PCT?

11. "There's no way to know what makes one thing happen and not another. . . . But I was pretty certain as I sat there that night that if it hadn't been for Eddie, I wouldn't have found myself on the PCT." How does this realization change Strayed's attitude towards her stepfather?

12. To lighten her load, Strayed burns each book as she reads it. Why doesn't she burn the Adrienne Rich collection?

Discover great *value* for your book club
with these *3-in-1 collections*!

COMING
NOVEMBER
2013

COMING
JANUARY
2014

Available Now

READ EXCERPTS FROM THESE BOOKS AND MORE
AT WWW.WATERBROOKMULTNOMAH.COM.

WATERBROOK MULTNOMAH
PUBLISHING GROUP
A DIVISION OF RANDOM HOUSE, INC.

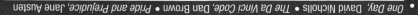

extremely witty conversation with southern authors
most excellent recommendations for reading
clever & refined musings of booksellers & writers
engaging & amusing author readings
illuminating excerpts from great southern books
and other such items as are of interest to
her ladyship, the editor

Lady Banks' Commonplace Book

front porch literary gossip
from your favorite southern bookshops

subscribe at ladybankscommonplacebook.com

BOOK GROUP RESOURCES

About reading groups and book clubs

- **ReadingGroupChoices.com**—Thousands of guides available plus giveaways and interactive materials for reading groups

- **Book-Clubs-Resource.com**—A guide to book clubs and reading groups with a collection of links and information for readers, including information about saving with discount book clubs

- **BookClubCookbook.com**—Recipes and food for thought from your book club's favorite books and authors

- **BookClubGirl.com**—Dedicated to sharing great books, news, and tips with book club girls everywhere

- **BookGroupBuzz.BooklistOnline.com**—Book group tips, reading lists, & lively talk of literary news from the experts at Booklist Online

- **NationalReadingGroupMonth.org**—Celebrating the joy of shared reading

- **LiteraryAffairs.net**—Book club picks and author events from one of the leading book club facilitators in the country

About Books

- **ShelfAwareness.com**—A free e-mail newsletter dedicated to helping the people in stores, in libraries and on the Web buy, sell, and lend books most wisely

- **GenerousBooks.com**—A community for those who love books and love to discuss them

- **BookMuse.wordpress.com**— Musings about books, readers, and making connections

- **BookBrowse.com**—Book reviews, excerpts, and author interviews

- **BookSpot.com**—Help in your search for the best book-related content on the Web

- **GoodReads.com**—Meet your next favorite book

READING GROUP *Choices*

We wish to thank the authors, agents, publicists, librarians, booksellers, and our publishing colleagues who have continued to support this publication by calling to our attention some quality books for group discussion, and the publishers and friends who have helped to underwrite this edition.

Algonquin

Amy Einhorn Books/ Putnam

Anchor

Gallery Books

Harlequin MIRA

Harmony

Harper Perennial

Houghton Mifflin Harcourt

Kensington Books

Koehler Books

Liveright

Other Press

Penguin Books

Riverhead

Rodale

Vintage

William Morrow

WW Norton

iPad App!

Reading Group Choices on your iPad!

Our FREE iPad app gives you and your book club all that **Reading Group Choices** has to offer right at your fingertips!

- FREE Book Drawings
- Conversation Starters
- Discussible Book Selections
- Push Notifications
- eBook Downloads
- eNewsletters
- *On the Bookcase* Blog
- Access to thousands of discussible books!

 **Reading Group Choices'** goal is to join with publishers, bookstores, libraries, trade associations, and authors to develop resources to enhance the shared reading group experience.

Reading Group Choices is distributed annually to bookstores, libraries, and directly to book groups. Titles from previous issues are posted on **ReadingGroupChoices.com**. Books presented here have been recommended by book group members, librarians, booksellers, literary agents, publicists, authors, and publishers. All submissions are then reviewed to ensure the discussibility of each title. Once a title is approved for inclusion by the Advisory Board (see below), publishers are asked to underwrite production costs, so that copies of *Reading Group Choices* can be distributed for a minimal charge.

For additional copies, please call your local library or bookstore, or contact us by phone or email. Quantities are limited. For more information, please visit our website at **ReadingGroupChoices.com**

READING GROUP CHOICES' ADVISORY BOARD

Donna Paz Kaufman founded the bookstore training and consulting group of Paz & Associates in 1992, with the objective of creating products and services to help independent bookstores and public libraries remain viable in today's market. A few years later, she met and married **Mark Kaufman**, whose background included project management, marketing communications, and human resources. Together, they launched **Reading Group Choices** in 1994 to bring publishers, booksellers, libraries, and readers closer together. They sold **Reading Group Choices** to Barbara and Charlie Mead in May 2005. They now offer training and education for new and prospective booksellers, architectural design services for bookstores and libraries, marketing support, and a training library for professional and staff development on a wide variety of topics. To learn more about Paz & Associates, visit PazBookBiz.com.

Neely Kennedy serves as the current *Literary Director* for **Reading Group Choices**. The love of collection development is the common thread that connects Neely's extensive experience in the book industry. A former librarian, she has worked in both public and academic libraries. From 2002–2007 she owned and operated The Wise Willow, a successful independent bookstore in historic downtown Annapolis, Maryland. Additionally, her position in Marketing and Publicity at the *Naval Institute Press* gained her knowledge of the inner workings of the publishing industry.

John Mutter is editor-in-chief of *Shelf Awareness*, the daily e-mail newsletter focusing on books, media about books, retailing and related issues to help booksellers, librarians and others do their jobs more effectively. Before he and his business partner, Jenn Risko, founded the company in May 2005, he was executive editor of bookselling at *Publishers Weekly*. He has covered book industry issues for 25 years and written for a variety of publications, including *The Bookseller* in the U.K.; *Australian Bookseller & Publisher*; *Boersenblatt*, the German book trade magazine; and *College Store Magazine* in the U.S. For more information about *Shelf Awareness*, go to its website, shelf-awareness.com.

Mark Nichols was an independent bookseller in various locations from Maine to Connecticut from 1976 through 1993. After seven years in a variety of positions with major publishers in New York and San Francisco, he joined the American Booksellers Association in 2000, and currently serves as Senior Director, Publisher Initiatives. He is on the Board of James Patterson's ReadKiddoRead.com, and has edited two volumes with Newmarket Press—*Book Sense Best Books* (2004) and *Book Sense Best Children's Books* (2005).

Nancy Olson has owned and operated Quail Ridge Books & Music in Raleigh, NC, since 1984, which has grown from 1,200 sq. ft. to 9,000+ sq. ft and sales of $3.2 million. The bookstore won three major awards in 2001: *Publishers Weekly* Bookseller of the Year, Charles Haslam Award for Excellence in Bookselling; Pannell Award for Excellence in Children's Bookselling. It was voted "Best in the Triangle" in the *Independent Weekly* and *Metro Magazine*.

Jill A. Tardiff is publishing industry consultant and project manager working under her banner company Bamboo River Associates. She is also advertising manager for such print and online publications as *Parabola —Tradition, Myth, and the Search for Meaning*, as well as contributing editor at *Publishers Weekly*. Jill is the past president of the Women's National Book Association (WNBA) and WNBA-New York City chapter, 2004–2006 and 2000–2005, respectively. She is currently WNBA's National Reading Group Month Committee Chair and Coordinator and its United Nations Department of Public Information NGO Chief Representative. She is currently working on several book proposals on modern-day pilgrimage.